KU-786-729

alexis caught

queer up

WALKER
BOOKS

WEST NORTHAMPTONSHIRE
COUNCIL

60000493305

Askews & Holts

KK

First published 2022 by Walker Books Ltd
87 Vauxhall Walk, London SE11 5HJ

2 4 6 8 10 9 7 5 3 1

Text © 2022 Alexis Caught
Illustrations © Walker Books Limited
Illustrations by Jamie Hammond

The right of Alexis Caught to be identified as author
of this work has been asserted by them in accordance
with the Copyright, Designs and Patents Act 1988

This book has been typeset in Futura T and Abril Fatface

Printed and bound by CPI Group (UK) Ltd, Croydon CR0 4YY

All rights reserved. No part of this book may be reproduced,
transmitted or stored in an information retrieval system in
any form or by any means, graphic, electronic or mechanical,
including photocopying, taping and recording, without prior
written permission from the publisher.

While Walker Books uses reasonable efforts to include up-to-
date information about resources available (including their
website addresses (URLs) included in this book), we cannot
guarantee accuracy and all such resources are provided
for informational purposes only.

British Library Cataloguing in Publication Data: a catalogue
record for this book is available from the British Library

ISBN 978-1-4063-9922-6

www.walker.co.uk

MIX
Paper from
responsible sources
FSC® C171272

WALKER
BOOKS

An Uplifting Guide to LGBTQ+ Love, Life and Mental Health

queer up

alexis caught

contents

Written by Charlie Craggs and Kuchenga

Hi there,

We're going to be getting to know one another pretty intimately in this book, so I suppose it's polite to start with an introduction. I'm Alexis (hi again), I'm a writer, podcaster, rugby player, Kate Bush obsessive, salted-over-sweet popcorn fan, pick-n-mix fiend and therapist. Throughout my life, I've always been interested in the tricky and complicated — and yet so fascinating and fun — area of our sexuality. I ended up in this line of work, and writing this book, because I've always had questions about my own sexuality (short version: I'm a gay man — but as you read on, you'll find it's a bit more nuanced than that), questions about others and where we fit into this world.

I'm guessing that you probably have a lot of questions, too, maybe about your sexuality and feelings, or maybe you're just generally interested in the world and others around you. Questions can be great and asking why is enjoyable, but there are also times in our lives when it feels super scary and quite overwhelming. When I was younger, I had a scary, confusing "why?" stage where I had so many questions about who I was, how I felt, why I felt like I did ... it was lonely.

That's what this book is here to do: make sure that you know you're not alone. I can't promise that this book will contain all the answers (and, to be honest, it shouldn't, because a lot of those answers come from within you) but I can promise that along with a wonderful bunch of people from all along the LGBTQ+ spectrum we are here in this book to support you, so you know that you are not alone.

Together, we'll look at big queer questions, along with specifics of love and sex, LGBTQ+ history (my fave nerd topic), dealing with other people (things such as coming out, navigating dating etc.) and plenty of practical mental health support and advice.

I'm not here as your mentor, definitely not as an all-knowing person who's got all their sh*t figured out (top tip: the more someone says they have all the answers the more likely it is they haven't fully understood the question) and certainly not as a role model (is anyone? Aren't we all just a bit too flawed for that?). I'm here as your friend, your big gay brother, your cheerleader, totally your equal who just happens to be a little bit further along the yellow brick road than you, shouting back some directions, drawing some arrows pointing to different things to look out for along the way and keeping you company on this journey.

I look forward to going on this adventure together.

alexis x

A note on language and time

Language, the words we use and how we refer to things changes. Sometimes it changes pretty fast, and sometimes two people's take on the use of a word will be polar opposites. As I write this book, I am acutely aware that my use of language and the terms used may one day change out of favour and be considered not the "right" thing to say. What I would say here, is that my own opinion is that we ask WHY are we so focused on the *word* and not the *intent* behind it. All words are made up, and are only interpretations of intended meaning. My intended meaning, with any words or phrases I use here, is never malicious, never wishing to leave anyone out, they're just the best fit that I currently have, but I apologize if anything makes you uncomfortable – that is never my intent.

As an example, I'm going to use the word "queer" a lot in this book, a word some people still have issues with. That word was spat at me as a slur (along with others, that I won't be using in these pages) but our community has taken it back, and (in my opinion) it gives us the power. We could bend and agree with any homophobic or transphobic people out there that *being queer* is a bad thing, or we could say: you know what? I am. We are. And that's our word. And we're going to show how BRILLIANT being that word is.

Our community has a great history of reclaiming these things (even our rainbow flag has its origins in reclaiming our power from homophobia).

So if anything I say in here offends or upsets you because of my use of language, I wholeheartedly apologize – your feelings are valid, if this were a conversation I'd apologize and use a different word right away. Unfortunately, the limitations of print mean I can't change it, but know that there is no malice in my intent. Similarly, when (inevitably) some of this book gets outdated and we move beyond some of the things written in here, I also apologize – it was the best at the time, and frankly, I can't wait until some stuff I've said is outdated and we've moved on to better places.

Shout

When writing this book I also wanted to partner with Shout — a free, confidential and totally non-judgemental text line that you can contact 24/7 to talk about how you feel. Shout is a brilliant charity, staffed by lots of open-minded, caring and compassionate people (I know personally, I'm one of the volunteers on the line!) who are available whenever, if ever, you may need a little more support. Just text 'SHOUT' to 85258 to start the conversation (see pages 244—245 for more information on Shout).

questioning

Breathe.

Just breathe.

There's a high chance that there are a lot of questions in your head right now, such as:

Phew! That's a lot of questions, and there's possibly a lot more. Perhaps even, "Oh God, what will they think of me if they see me reading this book?" So, for now, just breathe. You're gonna be OK.

In this book, we're not always going to be giving you straight answers, or even gay answers. We're here (and I really do mean "we", because I've enlisted a fantastic group of glittering people from all along the queer spectrum to give us their views and share their own life experiences, too) to help you find some of your own answers and navigate through when it all gets confusing. Sure, there will be pearls of wisdom, we'll share embarrassing mistakes and things we wish we'd not gone through – so that you don't have to make the same cringe mistakes (you're welcome, btw) – and there will be tips and tricks along the way.

But how can I help you? Well, one of the things I do with my time is work in the field of mental health. I talk a lot about feelings and help people figure out why we're here and what we're doing. But this book is *not* therapy. And, don't worry, it's also not going to be filled with unrealistic suggestions for wellness, such as wafting your nether regions with sage. What I will be sharing, though, is some practical tips for how to hack your head and check in on your emotions (a bit like when I reminded you to breathe just now). Everything is taken from my experience as a therapist and doing crisis intervention – keep an eye out for those 'Looking after you' advice and activity sections.

In the beginning, there was ... confusion?

Questions can be confusing. They can feel overwhelming and they can feel so numerous that the weight of them all stops us from thinking of anything else. But questions are also powerful. They're the ignition spark; the key in the engine for a journey of self-discovery. Having questions shows you are smart and that you are in tune with yourself. You have not just accepted the cookie-cutter template of "how to be" that society and tradition can sometimes place on us. So that's your first answer – no, you are not alone, it is "normal" to have questions and it is "normal" to be confused. You are not the first person to have questions about how you feel, about your body, about how you identify or who you are.

But let's get to a really big question... Are you queer? Are you lesbian? Trans? Gay? Bisexual? Perhaps none of those, but something else not quite straight?

I don't know. I can't tell you the answer to that. There's a chance that you might be. If so, firstly ... CONGRATULATIONS! (Caps lock intended, I mean that to be read as though I am shouting my excitement and congratulations to you!)

Welcome to the club, or rather, welcome to the family. I'm queer too, loads of us are. In fact, more and more people than ever are openly identifying as "other than the heterosexual-cisgender norm" (a really academic, boring phrase which I'll explain in just a moment) and more people are finding themselves somewhere under the rainbow in the LGBTQ+ family – or, queer, for short (that's how I'm going to be using it in this book).

But who and WHAT is the "LGBTQ+ community"?!

Sometimes known simply as LGBT, or LGBT+, LGBTQIA+, queer people or smaller groups, such as the gay community and the trans community – we're a proud, diverse and varied group of people, and all of us (in one way or another) identify as not entirely heterosexual ("straight") or cisgendered (identifying as being of the same gender we were assigned at birth). And together, we stand as a ragtag bunch under our rainbow banner, known as "the pride flag".

The name of the community is ever-changing and evolving as we broaden out our understanding of gender and sexual identities. No one name is right; no one name is wrong. Use what is best for you.

Our acronym frequently evolves, which I think is a great sign of us growing and expanding – not so long ago, we were even known by "GLBT", but after countless lesbian women looked after, campaigned for and acted as nurses for many gay men during the AIDS crisis, the L was moved first as a mark of respect to note their importance in our community.

The "L" to the "+" of the queer alphabet

Lesbian: a woman, who is attracted to other women

Gay: a man, who is attracted to other men

Bisexual: someone of any gender, attracted to both male and female genders

Transgender: people whose gender identity and expression differs from the gender that they were assigned at birth. Note: transgender does not imply anything on attraction, so trans people can identify as any sexuality

Transsexual: a word similar to transgender, but this implies medical changes to one's gender, such as surgery or hormones. It is best left for someone to identify themself by this term, if they so choose

Queer: anyone who isn't either straight or cisgender

Questioning: someone who isn't yet sure of their sexuality or gender and is taking some time to find themselves

Intersex: people who naturally (not through medical intervention) have biological gender traits that do not match with what is stereotypically understood as being male or female

Asexual: also known as "ace", this is an umbrella term for people who either don't experience any or experience little sexual attraction

Allies: people who identify as cisgender and heterosexual, and believe in the total social and legal equality for all queer people. Our most supportive friends and family can often sit here!

So, what about the "+"s?

Pansexual: a.k.a. "Pan" – people who are attracted to others regardless of their sex or gender identity. Is this the same as bisexuality? Some say yes, some say no, some say it specifically includes attraction to people with non-traditional gender expression. What matters is how people who identify as pansexual feel about it – that's all!

Demisexual: "demi" is when someone can only experience sexual attraction after an emotional bond. Like asexuality, anybody of any sexual orientation can experience this

Sapiosexual: the attraction to intelligence and the mind over gender

Agender: sometimes referred to as "genderless" or "ungendered" – it's exactly as it sounds! It's for people who identify as having no gender identity

Gender queer: there are a whole host of non-conforming gender identities and names such as gender queer, gender fluid, pangender, which includes people whose gender feels moveable, flexible and unfixed to them

This list is not definitive. These are not the only ways people do/can/should identity and there are many more identities than those stated here – but that's one of the wonders of life and the spectrum we live in. With SO many different colours and shades out there, you can choose to colour your life as best suits you.

What is the spectrum?

One of the ways that we can take the pressure off ourselves and make the big, scary questions of "What am I?", "Am I?" and "How will I know?" all a lot less heavy is by thinking in terms of spectrums rather than binaries. A binary, like in computers, is a choice between two things, such as black and white or one and zero, and traditional (outdated and old-fashioned) thinking would have us believe that we are faced with a binary choice of being either heterosexual or homosexual ... and that's it. One or the other. Of course, human sexuality and identity is waaaaaaaaay more complicated than that. That's why we like to think of sexuality and gender as a spectrum. Rather than thinking of it as either black or white, a spectrum would have the brightest shade of white at one end, and the deepest darkest shade of black at the other, with a multitude of shades and variants in the middle.

Don't worry if this still sounds confusing — that's precisely what this book is here to help with, and exactly why we've started with this chapter on questions.

Years of queers

Did you know that there is evidence of same-sex attraction, desire and marriage from the ancient world? A diary entry of an Ancient Egyptian priestess and small statues of a same-sex couple have shown same-sex unions existed in older civilisations. The skeletons of two men discovered in Italy, believed to be a same-sex couple, known as the Lovers of Modena, were found holding hands and are almost 3,000 years old. There was even an Ancient Roman sort-of gay bar discovered in the ruins of Pompeii, recently identified by the translations of writing at the site which referred to homosexual patrons.

Similarly, trans people have been present in ancient cultures across the world. In the Czech Republic in 2011, the grave of what could well be the oldest example of a trans person was discovered: archaeologists found a 5,000-year-old burial site, where the skeleton had been buried as a woman, with burial gifts and commemorations typically associated with women's graves, yet the skeleton was genetically male.

We've gone by many different names, including sometimes with no names at all, but what we now broadly describe as the LGBTQ+ community has always been here. We're not new. We're not going away. And we're part of a rich, long legacy.

But what do these labels mean to me?

It's helpful to have an understanding of what these terms mean because it is an important thing to many people. It can help us better understand where we're each coming from and to understand each other better. But the terms we use to identify ourselves, the pronouns we use, the labels we choose to use (or not) are not the entire story and do not define who we are — they're just the blurb. All that fun and fascinating narrative and character development happens in the pages as we write our own story.

So yes, it is important to know what these things mean, but it's also really important to not feel heavily weighed down by them, or like you have to force yourself into a box. You are entirely free to choose not to label yourself. Rather than see each other through defined labels, we should see it as a rough guide and allow all of us to determine what that means for us, and express it however we feel.

For me, I refer to myself as LGBTQ+ or queer. Some people don't like the term queer, because it did get co-opted and used as a slur against us, but it's actually a very old term for our community and, as it's been reclaimed, many of us have grown to love it again. This is why I really like the term queer — it gives us all some flexibility and freedom! But that is *my* preference! Our community has a long history of reclaiming things (the pride flag, the pink triangle), so I embrace the power in reclaiming queer.

In terms of my own identity, I shape it for myself. I identify as a gay man, who sits within the queer spectrum. On paper, if we take the "box ticking" approach, that means I am exclusively male and exclusively attracted to other males. But the reality is I've had romantic, emotional and sexual relationships and encounters with both men and women, and people who are trans and gender queer. My own gender remains fluid – I've been incredibly androgynous in my time (meaning I displayed characteristics of both sexes, wearing "male" and "female" clothing, where people haven't been able to "gender" me by appearance). These days, I've got muscles and stubble because I enjoy the presentation of this "man drag", yet feel happily more feminine inside. I know my insides – my spirit, heart, head and essence – are pretty fluid and would fall into a non-binary/gender fluid camp. My mum can remember when I was four or five and would rush home from school to put on a dress and suddenly relax – it's just an innate part of me, even though now I predominantly wear "male-assigned" clothing and look more masculine because (despite the old saying) the clothes *don't* make the man.

The important thing is that you go at your own pace, and work out who you are inside and how you want to live, moving towards creating peace between the two. As I said before, *what* you are matters less than *who* you are. You are you, loveable and special – identifying one way or another isn't going to change that.

Of course, you might not be queer — perhaps you've picked up this book because you've seen it on a bookshelf and your questions are about the lives and experiences of other people. That's cool, too — in fact, having an interest in other people and wanting to learn how you can better support those people is *the coolest* thing. Straight people who are like this are known as "allies" and throughout this book, you'll find little 'Advice for allies' sections. Now, of course, queer people can also be allies. For example, a lesbian cisgender woman can be an ally to a heterosexual trans woman. That's like backing up your sibling and looking out for your family members or best mates.

What if you just don't know? What if you don't know where you fit in and you're not quite sure what's going on with your emotions, thoughts and feelings? That, too, is absolutely OK. For some people (like me) their queerness was just an ever-present part of them. Like a lot of nine-year-old boys, I loved the Power Rangers, except ... ya know ... I *really* loved the Power Rangers. For others, it's a slower, more gradual experience or, for some, it was like a lightning bolt out of nowhere. We're all unique and, because we're all different, the way that we grow into ourselves is different for everyone. Our sexuality and our identity is not just a spectrum, it is a limitless cosmos of opportunity to express how you feel — and shine brightly for it.

Looking after you: how to handle overwhelming questions

When we have a million questions running around our heads, particularly when they feel heavy and important, it can feel overwhelming. The advice I'm sharing with you here will help you cope when you are feeling worried or upset, whether it's stress about the questions in this book or even exams at school.

- **Acknowledge and accept the feelings:** Take a second to pause and just think – how are you feeling? Anxious? Stressed? Nervous? Scared? That is OK. These aren't particularly nice feelings, but they are a reality of life and an inescapable part of being human. Stop exhausting yourself by fighting off these emotions or making yourself feel guilty for how you feel. Acknowledge how you feel and remind yourself that it's OK.

> I feel pretty stressed right now. That's understandable. I haven't been through this before — it's normal to feel nervous about something you don't know.

- **Reframe your thoughts:** It can sometimes be a little tough to think of a way to reframe things that feel bad or scary, and it's not as simple as "cancelling out", but think of it as consciously choosing to change the channel. Whenever a show you don't like is on TV, you can change the channel. Sure, your favourite show might not be on either but it's better than before. We can try to change how we view the thoughts that are worrying us and move towards feeling better and more positive.

> OK, I don't have all of the answers right now. That's confusing. But I'm going to get them, and I'll know so much more about myself. I can't wait to see how I grow.

- **Remember to breathe:** It can sound silly reminding people to breathe – it's something we do instinctively. Except, we don't. Sometimes, when we're stressed, we can unconsciously hold our breath or take shallow breaths. Breathing deeply makes your body and brain relax. When you feel stressed, try to relax your shoulders, breathing slowly and deeply.

> **How are my shoulders feeling? How's my breathing? I'll feel better if I slow this down and just breathe.**

- **Live in the moment:** It's understandable to worry about the future. When there are so many unknown answers, never-ending questions and endless possibilities, we can feel overwhelmed by scary "what if?" questions. We can trick ourselves that thinking ahead to them will help us plan, but, actually, it just exhausts us. If you're feeling emotionally overwhelmed by future events or thoughts, try to focus on the present. Look around you and remind yourself where you are.

> **I'm worried about what's ahead. It's scary. But if I focus on where I am right now, I'll feel more grounded. I can tackle what's coming.**

Big queer questions

Now that we've equipped ourselves with ways to handle our thoughts when the pressure of unanswered questions gets too much, how about we look at some of those BIG questions together?

When did you first know?

It's a question so many queer people get asked. Sometimes it's a glib and pithy answer: "When did I realize that I was a lesbian? When I realized the alternative was straight men!" (Courtesy of a mate of mine.) Other times it's a more thoughtful answer, "I realized that the feelings I had for a friend went beyond wanting them to be my best, best friend, and suddenly realizing that I was in love with another man." (An answer from a teammate of mine.) Knowing we're somewhere in the LGBTQ+ spectrum is one thing, and many of us do have moments where the realization formed and we levelled up in our understanding and knowledge of ourselves. But before that, there comes questioning.

How will I know?

Is it OK to feel like this?

What am I?

Is feeling like this normal?

What if?

And yes, we even ask ourselves sometimes, will this go away?

There are, of course, lots of other questions that we'll come to throughout this book, but for now, let's start with these ones and have a little look one by one.

What if?

Well, what if you are? Does it change who you are as a person? Does it make you odd? Does it make you the only one? Does it mean anything bad? The answer to all these questions is a resounding, warm and comforting "no". Being anywhere on the LGBTQ+ spectrum means nothing bad. It does not make you a different person. You are still you — just in bold, bright colour.

What am I?

There's no easy answer. I can't "diagnose" you from afar. You shouldn't feel pressured into accepting a label that others are putting on you for their own convenience and comfort. Ultimately, it matters less about *what* you are and more about *who* you are — and however you identify, who you are doesn't change. You may fancy people of the same gender, you might fancy nobody, you might fancy both genders — and speaking of gender, you might question your own or feel as though you have none. Don't rush to label it, just take your time and be open to exploring your heart and mind.

Perhaps you've had some new feelings arise after seeing a scene in a new film that has led to some interesting daydreams about one of the characters, and that got your brain asking questions... Perhaps it was realizing that, hang on, you *like-like* a friend. Perhaps it was wearing nail varnish "as a joke" and something feeling right. This might sound odd – but you'll *know* when you're ready to accept yourself and it'll make sense. And speaking of acceptance...

Is it OK to feel like this?

Absolutely. That I can answer for you – yes, one hundred, ten thousand per cent – yes, it *is* OK. It might still feel scary, but being queer, any way that you identify, is absolutely OK. There are complications, admittedly, sometimes our background and culture can play a role in making us feel like we're bringing shame on ourselves or our family and friends, but it will all still be OK.

Religion can also play a part as, due to how long ago religious texts were written, they can have very outdated views on tolerance and acceptance of others. (Don't forget, the Bible even banned shellfish at one point.) But times do change. The Christian church has begun a journey towards modernization. Judaism has seen many high-profile rabbis speak in favour of LGBTQ+ equality, while Islam has seen many imams do the same. If you are struggling, there are queer religious support groups for people who are struggling to come to terms with their faith and their heart. Check our support guide at the back of the book for specific faith resources.

Is it normal?

A recent study of census data showed that the LGBTQ+ community makes up roughly one in ten of the general population. That's the same percentage of the population that is left-handed. Just because people who are left-handed do things slightly differently doesn't mean they're not normal – and the same goes for us. In fact, another study has suggested it is more likely to be one in seven of the population identify as LGBTQ+, meaning there are MORE of us than left-handers!

And it's not just the human world – there are gay animals too! SERIOUSLY! Google the gay penguins at Sydney Zoo in Australia or at London Zoo. Similarly, there are trans animals, non-binary animals and animals that don't match up to the narrow definition of male or female characteristics – male sea horses are the ones that give birth! So yes – we are "normal".

Will this go away?

This answer is an odd one. Our sexual and gender identity is not a phase, not something we'll "grow out of". But there is a slight caveat here — there are some people who, with a rush of puberty hormones, do experience momentary same-sex attraction. If we think back to the LGBTQ+ spectrum, maybe they'd be an "E," for "Exploring". For those people, a passing attraction is just that — passing. But this in no way means that our identity is "just a phase" that will go away. But nor should it, there's nothing wrong with who we are, how we feel or who we love. What will go away, and I promise you this, is any fear or concern that you may be holding. That goes away and leaves in its place confidence, acceptance, power and pride.

Embracing growth

As we live our lives, we want to grow and evolve. Personal growth and development are rooted in being open to change and (you can probably guess the next bit) to change, we have to be open to questions. As a therapist, my most important job is helping people feel secure and supported as they ask themselves big questions about their lives: Are they happy? What do they want? How would they like to be known and remembered? What will make them feel whole?

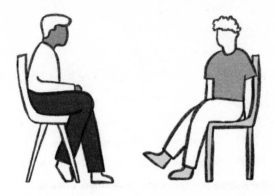

To find the answers to these questions, to live our lives as fully as possible, we have to stay open to new experiences and questions. Think of it like food – sure, you've got your favourites that you know you enjoy, but one day you ask yourself, "I wonder what that's like?" and try something new. Asking questions about ourselves is how we find new, enjoyable flavours to bring into our lives.

Some of the most interesting people I know are the ones who still ask big questions about themselves well into their 50s, 60s and 70s, and even beyond. The coolest people I know are the ones who are always open to questions of new feelings and adventures. How boring and limited would life be if we only ate one thing and were never open to tasting new flavours?!

People who are more open have what's known as a growth mindset, and are often happier embracing life and its challenges. People who have a closed mindset, where they see themselves as being fixed at birth, often struggle to find the opportunity for development and growth. Embrace your questions and stay open to your own evolution, because getting to know ourselves is a life's work.

Queer and questioning

Ryan Lanji, Cultural Producer and Presenter (he/him)

People always ask me when I knew I was queer and I immediately retort with, "Well, when did you know you were straight?" I've always been open to what is unknown, but I distinctly remember when I found out about the word 'gay' and seeing the reactions of the way people regarded it sent me into a spiral cloaked by optimism. It's been a journey (especially being south Asian).

Kayza Rose, Film-maker and Founding Director of BLM Fest (blmfest.co.uk) (she/her)

I must have been around seven or eight years old. I had this fascination with this other girl in my class, she was new to the school. I just wanted to be near her, loved the way she looked, everything about her was amazing to me. I knew I didn't just want to be her friend and I didn't want to be her. I didn't have the language for it at that time or know exactly what it meant but there she was, and she was everything to me.

Masuma Rahim, Clinical Psychologist (she/her)

There are more ways to interpret scripture than you'd believe — and God and faith mean different things to everyone. Your relationship with faith may ebb and flow, but there is a place for you at the table, if you want it. It can be tempting to be furious at a faith that you're told doesn't accept you, but it's always possible to reevaluate your relationship, and there will always be people within that faith group who will welcome you, love you and accept you.

Chris Bryant, Comedian and Designer (they/he/she)

I find it funny that a rainbow and spectrum are both used as symbols of gender, sexuality and autism. I truly feel like my whole life is on a spectrum, and that the more I learn about myself and how my brain functions the more questions I have. I've had to find comfort and patience in uncertainty. Life and growth is an iterative process, and there is beauty in the undefined. Sometimes people can't quickly categorize me or put me in a box, and that may frustrate them. I've learned to place boundaries and not take the brunt of other's frustration.

Teddy Edwards, Producer and LICK Events Founder (she/her)

I remember being in primary school and my friends having crushes on celebrity men and thinking, "God, I really just fancy Shania Twain?"

Marc Thompson, Director of The Love Tank (thelovetank.info) and Co-founder of PrEPster (prepster.info) and Black & Gay Back in the Day (he/him)

I was aware that I liked boys around age ten, but I didn't have the language or words to describe my feelings until I was about thirteen or fourteen. Whilst I wasn't confused about my sexuality I did go through a short period when I didn't want to be gay because I thought it would be a lonely life. I was a teenager in the 80s, so finding books or films where I could see myself was incredibly limited. I discovered gay porn and some gay magazines, such as Gay Times, in my early teens. This gave me an outlet and an understanding that I wasn't alone in the world.

Advice for allies

How was reading all of that? Did it raise questions for you about how you "knew" you were heterosexual? Has it raised any questions for you about your own experiences of attraction or how you feel about your gender?

As you can see, there are lots of BIG questions that can be going through people's heads. Deep, existential questions that can carry a lot of weight with them. That's why it's important that as allies – as friends, as family – we give people space, time and our unconditional support. By picking up this book and engaging, you're already on your way to doing that.

the T in LGB...

Written by **Charlie Craggs** and **Kuchenga**

Within the ever-expanding alphabet soup of the LGBTQ+ directory, there are many different identities and sexualities. But prominently within our acronym (and within our history and culture) is the T for transgender. While being transgender is not about sexual attraction and is about gender identity, trans people have long been an important part of our community and story.

In order to explain (or worse, "justify") why the T is welcome within our LGB family, I could make the common argument about how trans people have always been vital figures in queer rights movements, and that's true, but trans people deserve respect, solidarity and support not because of what they've done or achieved, but because they are human and we are all deserving of rights. We can't argue for our own LGB freedoms, equalities and protections and leave some behind — that's not fighting for equality, that's just fighting for preferential treatment while being happy to exclude others. That's why we also

have to be active against racism, misogyny, xenophobia and ableism and make a stand against all types of discrimination. Equality for some is not good enough, it has to be equality for all. Trans people deserve our solidarity and a place in our movement because they are people, and we are stronger, shining brighter together.

And although I just mentioned our community's story, this particular chapter isn't my own story to tell. While I don't identify as entirely cisgender, considering myself to be much more non-binary, it's an important lesson for us all to not seek to lead every conversation on queer issues, to not lead every parade, to sometimes take a step back and hand the microphone to others, acknowledging that there is space and a place for us all. With this in mind, I want to introduce you to two brilliant women I know so that you can hear from their wealth of wisdom, knowledge and infectious humour and spirit.

I give you Charlie and Kuchenga.

Hi!

My name is **Kuchenga**.

My father told me when I was growing up that my name meant protector of the village, which sounds rather grandiose. I have since met other Zimbabweans who have told me my name means something completely different. Nevertheless, I have always taken my responsibilities to my communities quite seriously.

I am a Black trans woman. The cards I was dealt meant the path to a healthy life has been treacherous. There have been so many times when I did not think I would make it through certain experiences. However, I am glad to report that because of the love and support of people who share my identity – and our allies – I have come to believe that I deserve and will lead a long healthy life.

I read Black feminist literature as a matter of survival, and, because of the example of Black women writers, in adulthood I was compelled to become involved with organizations that improved the lives of others. I have written to trans girls in prison, worked for Black queer trans liberation and volunteered for homeless organizations. In doing so, I have received much more than I have given. I now see my writing as a form of activism and hope that my work brings comfort, affirmation and hope to as wide a range of people as possible.

Hey!

My name is **Charlie Craggs**, I'm a trans activist and author and, for the purpose of Lex's amazing book, your big sister, along with my sister Kuchenga.

I started getting involved with trans activism early on in my transition back in 2013, because it was a very different time back then, before we had the trans representation we do today and the only time you saw a trans person in the media would be when they were being attacked. We were only ever punchlines or punching bags.

I'm probably best known for the campaign I run, Nail Transphobia, where I travel around the UK with my pop-up nail salon and squad of trans nail techs offering the public free manicures for the chance to sit down and have a chat with a real trans person in a bid to break misconceptions and make allies.

I also have a book called *To My Trans Sisters* and a BBC documentary called *Transitioning Teens*.

All my work in the media and on social media revolves around educating people about trans stuff, and that's what Lex has invited me to do here with Kuchenga. And in the way that I hope people leave my pop-up nail salon with a better understanding of trans people and issues, I hope you leave this chapter with the same.

Charlie: So we met on the set of a project for the BBC about six years ago. It's crazy how our lives have changed since then. We were little trans babies at the start of our journeys. I'm so proud of how far we've come!

Kuchenga: We were so raw and fragile. Early transition requires so much courage. I remember feeling like we could breathe into each other's pain because, at the time, the streets were a war zone. The harassment and violence we endured was so intense that when we were around each other we could really relax into ourselves. The phrase and notion of a safe space is sometimes derided in public conversation, but that's what we gave each other. A sisterly haven from the storm.

Charlie: Yeah, for sure. The next time we connected, you invited me to your place for dinner one evening to hang out properly. I remember, on the bus to yours, I realized it was Valentine's Day and started panicking. Was it a date? Hahaha. But it was such a nice evening and the start of our friendship.

Kuchenga: Well, in a way it was a date! Even though our relationship is platonic, I definitely wished to form a bond between us that would endure. I knew how much I wished to depend on you. I wanted to be able to call you out of the blue for long emotional conversations. I went to get the good chicken thighs from Marks & Spencer, seasoned them up the night before. Lit a candle from The Sanctuary to set the mood and everything. The coming together of a trans coven has a certain romance to it.

Charlie: That night was monumental for me. It was the first time I had ever hung out and talked with another trans girl properly. It showed me the importance of that. Like how we had so much shared experience, the same love for the YouTube series *T-Time With The Gurlz*. We had so many of the same struggles with being so early on in our transitions and getting abuse and stuff. It was so validating.

Kuchenga: Yeah, because we gave our trauma context and encouraged each other to believe in a better life being achievable and very much round the corner.

Charlie: You were definitely my first trans sister. Now here we are being big sisters to everyone reading this!

What's the 101?

Let's go back to basics. "Trans" is basically an umbrella term for people who are gender non-conforming. The gender we are assigned at birth comes with certain expectations. If your behaviour doesn't conform to what is expected of your assigned gender at birth, you are quite simply gender non-conforming.

The term is most commonly used for "transgender" people – people who do not feel comfortable with the gender they are assigned at birth and who may wish to take steps to medically and surgically fix that problem. However, "trans" can also cover a range of gender-variant identities such as non-binary people or drag queens – people who don't feel that comfortable in the gender (and thus the gender roles) they were assigned at birth.

Within this spectrum, there are all sorts of "non-traditional" (i.e. minority) genders and expressions – anybody who doesn't fit the definition of cisgendered.

There's a difference between sex and gender. Sex is more scientific, it's defined by a set of biological characteristics – like having a vagina and breasts – whereas gender is more of a feeling: it's how you dress, how you act, how you talk, what you like. It's not based on fact or science, it's personal.

One of the confusing things is that being trans doesn't actually have anything to do with being gay – except that we are part of the same LGBTQ+ community. You can be trans and be straight or gay or bi, or whatever. Your gender is totally separate from your sexuality – trans/cis is your gender and being queer/straight is your sexuality, you can be any combination of the two. The simplest way to understand it is that your sexuality is who you fancy and find attractive and your gender is how you view your body.

Charlie: If anyone ever does try to argue with you that being gay is a choice, please inform them that, since I transitioned, I am sadly now technically straight, quite the disappointment. Heterosexuality is not a choice or I'd choose to be gay! Similarly, being trans is not a choice, I don't think I know a single trans person that would choose to be trans. Don't get me wrong, I'm very proud to be trans, and happy to be so, but it has made my life so much harder. I overcome it, I thrive in spite of it, but it has to be acknowledged.

Breaking the binary

Just like sexuality is a spectrum of black and white with a whole lotta grey in the middle, it's key that we look at gender this way too and escape the idea that there are only two genders: male and female. Looking at gender (or even sexuality for that matter) in a rigid black and white way hurts everyone, even people who are (as they like to call themselves) "normal" (or as I like to call them ... "boring").

The gender binary is wrapped up with strict rules about what men and women can and can't do, and who we should all be. The idea that men have to be tough and manly hurts all men, not just men who are more "feminine", but also the tough and manly men because it puts them in a prison where they can't show emotion or have feelings and are policed if they do. This is why moving towards a society that lets everyone just be who they want and act how they want without judgement would help us all and is what we should be striving for.

On this note, it's also important to understand that when we talk about "trans" being an umbrella term for gender non-conforming people, being a man who is effeminate doesn't make you trans ... unless you feel it does, if that makes sense. It's kinda like an opt-in system. Language and labels are important for people to find words to explain how they feel and find people who feel a similar way to them but we shouldn't throw these labels onto other people.

To explain further, if a straight person kisses someone of the same sex that doesn't make them gay if they don't feel it does – it's a kiss, it's not that deep. Similarly, if you're a guy who likes wearing makeup or dresses or whatever, that doesn't make you trans, it makes you a guy who likes wearing makeup or dresses or whatever. Again, it's not that deep. A dress is a piece of clothing, not an identity. What we're trying to say is there's only one way to know if you're trans and that's if you know you're trans.

Kuchenga: I knew I was trans from a super young age. I was three or four and in nursery. There was a fierce black lace and purple satin nightie that I insisted on wearing and playing in every day. Obviously, it was "just a dress" but for me, it was part and parcel of the girl's world I longed to be a part of permanently and was a peaceful and blissful way of me expressing my gender as a young child before things got more complicated and upsetting.

Charlie: It was the same for me. I think a lot of us realize we're trans, or at least different than other boys and girls, around this age because it's the age we start being policed around our gender, especially in school. For example, being told we have to wear gendered uniforms or clothes, have to use gendered toilets and have to play with gendered toys or we'll be policed by our peers and teachers and told "that's not what boys/girls do". Like you, I used to play dress up in girls' clothes at home and didn't realize it wasn't "normal" until I went to nursery and was laughed at and told boys don't wear dresses by another kid. I didn't have a word for how I felt. I didn't know what trans meant or that it was even possible to transition, but I knew I wasn't like the other boys.

Years of queers

Did you know that other cultures have historically recognized multiple genders? There is evidence of third-gendered people (people who exist between male and female) existing in most ancient cultures. Trans people in these ancient cultures, such as the Two Spirit people of Native American culture, for example, were respected and revered members of society, often holding important roles such as healers, and were seen to be special beings who embodied both the masculine and the feminine. It was only when Colonial Christian forces invaded these ancient cultures and taught them that trans people (and gay people) were wrong that we were shunned from society. We have been fighting these beliefs and fighting for respect ever since.

Cultures all over the world recognized us, from the waria of Indonesia to the hijra in India. Even here in Britain and Northern Europe we have our own ancient examples of this. Followers of *seidh* (the Norse religion found here before Christianity) believed that some people were both male and female (called Ergi and Argr), and whose gods (you've heard of Loki!) changed gender at ease. There are even many trans animals, such as the clownfish, for example – Nemo is an unsung trans icon!

The documentation of trans-ness in nature and history really illustrates how it's such a natural part of life.

An introduction to terminology

Charlie: Language is important. The people who don't understand this and make fun of our community's terminology have probably never felt hurt or excluded by language. People like this often feel there shouldn't even be a word to explain being cisgender because it's "normal", but that would be like saying that there shouldn't be a word for being straight. Saying you're "normal" is saying people that aren't like you are abnormal, and that ain't cute. You shouldn't have to be from a certain community, know someone from that community or even understand that community to *respect* that community.

Kuchenga: And it's so easy too, let us help you out with some basic trans terminology.

Gender: a feeling, and a way of classifying people, based on more cultural and social constructed characteristics and differences, like the way we dress, act, talk and walk

Gender dysphoria: a feeling of discomfort and unhappiness around your gender/gendered body parts

Gender non-conforming: someone who, like the term suggests, breaks gendered norms around how they present and act

Non-binary/NB/gender fluid: a term for people who identify outside the realms of traditional gender roles such as male and female, and even 'drag queens' who dress up in the opposite gender's clothes be it for performance or pleasure. Either way the umbrella term trans is basically the different shades of grey between the black and white of male and female

Sex: a biological way of classifying people, based on their genitals

AFAB: assigned female at birth

AMAB: assigned male at birth

Transgender: a term for people who don't identify as the gender they were assigned at birth, and so socially (and often medically) transition afterwards so that their inner and external identity match up

Transition: the process (which is usually, but not exclusively, medical) of changing genders and/or sexes

MTF: male to female

FTM: female to male

Transsexual: a person whose transition is surgical, as the name implies the changing of sex

Crossdresser: a person who dresses up in the style of the opposite gender often for sexual enjoyment

Drag queen/king: a person who dresses up in the style of the opposite gender for performance

GCS: gender confirmation surgery – generally referring to lower surgery for transgender people

FFS: a series of procedures a person can have to feminize their face, undoing the effects of male puberty

FMS: a series of procedures a person can have to masculinize their face, undoing the effects of female puberty

Top surgery: surgery on the chest area, to either add breasts for trans women or remove them for trans men

Bottom surgery: surgery on the genitals, either changing a vagina into a penis or a penis into a vagina

So ... how does it feel?

It's hard to explain how you know you're trans. It's like trying to describe a colour, or the taste of water – it's a voice that comes from inside, something you just know at your core. There are similarities with how people may begin to sense they are gay. The authors and podcasters Tom & Lorenzo, who wrote the excellent book *Legendary Children: The First Decade of RuPaul's Drag Race and the Last Century* of *Queer Life*, pointed out that gay, queer and trans kids may all have that sense that we are "different" somehow, even though our final destinations when it comes to comfort with our identities may end up being wildly divergent. It's something you come to sense and know about yourself. How do you know? You just know. It's who you are. I guess put most simply, it's a feeling of discomfort in your assigned gender.

Kuchenga: For me as a trans kid and teen, having so many girl friends who were equally obsessed with pop music and culture was an absolute dream. I gravitated towards the impossibly sweet and sassy innocence of the pop girls of that moment: the Spice Girls, Britney Spears, Christina Aguilera and, of course, Destiny's Child. There was such an air of girl power and inspirational young womanly energy to revel in. Growing up, no matter my physical circumstances, I just knew that women's culture and media was for me, too. I made sure to pay attention and took in all the messaging about what it meant to 'be' a girl. This contributed immensely to my growing sense of self and made me the woman I am today.

Charlie: For me, the first realization wasn't so much realizing that I was trans (because I didn't know being trans was even a thing till I was a teenager) but more realizing I definitely wasn't a boy. A big part of this realization was to do with clothes and how I presented to the world: I felt SO uncomfortable in boys' clothes, which is ironic because boy clothes (and even just being a boy in general) are much more comfortable than stereotypically female clothes/ expectations, but it just didn't feel *right*. I felt like I was in drag – like I was performing at being a boy. It was so unnatural to me, a feeling of wishing I was the opposite gender. At four years old, I would pray I'd wake up a girl and would be devastated and in pain when I would wake up still in the body of a boy.

During puberty, I had this feeling of disgust when my body started changing in ways that weren't right for me. I hated myself. This is why it's a feeling that's hard to explain to anyone because you really won't need to explain it to anyone who is trans because it's a feeling you can't avoid or ignore. We all know it. I guess the best way to explain it to someone who isn't trans is to ask them how they know they're cis. They can't explain it – they just know they are. Going back to the gay comparison, it would be like when a straight person asks you how you know you're gay, to turn around and ask them how they knew they were straight. YOU JUST KNOW!

Kuchenga: What do I love about being trans? The strength, effervescence and integrity it takes to be unabashedly me. When I realized how much animosity there was in the world towards trans people, the fear made me recoil. I hid my true being from the world, but I cooked up plans for myself. Since then, I have grasped for everything the world had told me I would never get. I wanted to be loved, celebrated and welcomed into spaces where I had been told I would never belong. In reaching to meet those ambitions, I had to become unapologetic about taking up some deserved space. There is a very singular serenity that comes from achieving contentment with my body and my gender expression. In my gender transition, I have exceeded my own expectations. The moments of glory have been plentiful and, moreover, the connections I have made with people have shifted my understanding of what is possible for humanity in general.

Charlie: The best part about being trans for me is that I never thought it would be possible. Like I said, I didn't even know being trans was possible so the idea of getting to be the person I always felt inside was just a dream. My dream came true. Sometimes, when I'm doing basic everyday things, like doing my makeup ready for work, I get this excited, childish feeling in my chest. It's the greatest feeling in the world, a literal dream come true.

Advice for allies

One of the hardest things about being trans is how other people treat you, especially if this negativity or hurt comes from friends and family, or even just people who don't *intend* to be hurtful. As we know, though, it's not always about intent, it's about the impact and often the subtle or indirect microaggressions we face in our everyday lives as trans people that add up to cause massive impact.

Sadly, as trans people, we can face intrusive questions about very personal and traumatic parts of ourselves. If someone is worried about offending us and adding to this impact, the best advice is to question whether they'd ask or do what they're about to do to someone who *isn't* trans. For example, you wouldn't ask someone who isn't trans about their genitalia so don't ask us about ours! If a married woman tells you her new name, you'd accept it as that. You wouldn't ask her what her "real name" (maiden name) is. When she changes her name, people don't make a fuss about getting used to it like they do when trans people change names.

Trans people don't want special rights, we want human rights, we just want to be treated like everyone else. This is all people need to remember — if you wouldn't ask anyone else that question, don't ask us. And for the questions you *really* need to ask but are worried they might be offensive, you can find reliable resources at the back of this book.

Bullying and transphobia

Being trans is pretty easy. As we said, it's how we're treated by other people for being trans that's harder. Sadly, there's nothing we can say to make going through that sort of stuff any less difficult, but hopefully hearing us talk about it, knowing that it's something we all face, makes it slightly easier to bear. Every single trans person who has come before you has gone through the same and if they can — SO CAN YOU!

Historically, being different from others has been really dangerous for many people. People fear what they do not know and understand or have first-hand experience of. That fear means that bullying has been a feature of many a young trans person's life. It is so important that everyone knows that no one deserves to become a victim of violence. You deserve to feel safe and never have your boundaries compromised. We all deserve to have our dignity not be diminished by the actions of others. Your path to self-love is urgent. Transphobia tries to convince us that we are unworthy. This is not the case. You ARE worthy!

Dysphoria

Dysphoria — the sense that sex characteristics cause pain because of a discord with the body you were born into and the way you see yourself — is a mutating beast. At one point in your life, you might not pay much attention to your sex characteristics — then WHAM! — who you see when you look in the mirror makes your heart plummet, even if you have taken steps to help affirm your gender and are feeling mighty fine, having altered your appearance and how you are perceived in society. Still, one person can say something jarring or you see another trans person endure something that feels like it is happening to you — and BAM! — you are in touch with a raw pain that you hoped you would never have to feel again.

It is at these moments that it is fundamental to remember that we are all we have. You may feel lost at sea, but if you share your distress, a lifeboat can be sent out to bring

you back to shore. It could be as simple as a conversation. Remember, nothing lasts for ever and that this too shall pass. Have faith that the future always has the promise of being better than today. You can make it through.

Looking after you: coping tips

If you're reading this and you're trans, first of all, WELCOME TO THE FAMILY! We thought we'd give you some tips for how to affirm your gender and feel more comfortable in yourself during the early stages, especially if you're on one of the distinctly long waiting lists (that both of us have been on) to get on hormones or if you're too young to get on them. Either way, here are a few things we did to help us feel more comfortable in ourselves.

- **Exercise:** As well as a positive impact on your mental health (which might help during this time), there are exercises you can do to masculinize or feminize your body, like squats to grow that booty if you're a trans girl or bulking up your biceps to create a more top-heavy shape if you're a trans guy.

- **Saving:** Transition can be expensive so start saving money for future procedures now. Even if you're a million miles from where you want to be physically, if you start saving today, you'll feel like you're doing something active and productive to improve your future.

- **Practice:** Use this time to practise things like feminizing or masculinizing the way you talk, walk, dress and do your hair and makeup, etc. You learn by experimenting so start today. You can get your awkward phase out the way.

- **Community:** Do what you can to find your tribe. It's a pivotal time and the support will be invaluable. If you can't find them in real life, social media can be a great way of finding your tribe, but remember to stay safe.

- **Self-love:** Really try to work on your relationship with yourself during this time. Transition is hard, especially in the early days so you're going to need a strong and steady foundation. There's so much emphasis on the physical side of our transitions but if you're unhappy with who you are inside, you'll still be unhappy even after all the surgery in the world.

Being the other

Transgender people are a minority. As a result, we find ourselves being the only trans person someone cisgender can speak to or get to know. Being "the other" means that you might find yourself being in the position of being questioned and interrogated about being trans. In this position it can feel like you have to speak as if you represent the whole transgender community even though those of us who identify as transgender, non-binary, gender non-conforming are a really diverse group.

People will ask when you knew you were trans and how you knew. This can feel like an interrogation at times, as if you have to justify your otherness. On hearing others define themselves as transgender, non-binary, gender non-conforming you may feel close to them because their sense of themselves relates to how you relate to yourself. Awkwardly, you may find yourself feeling very distant from people who might share similar identity markers as you do.

The transgender umbrella

Some of us feel femme, masc, both or neither. Some of us see our gender identities as having a beginning and an endpoint; that we manifest divine femininity or sublime masculinity and go through life enjoying the personhood we fought to enjoy. Others may see themselves as fluid and constantly evolving; they shape-shift and mutate into new states of being with their journey through changing genders being a gorgeous example of beautiful anarchy and strength through a chaotic and complex approach to their sense of self.

In moving away from binary gender identities towards a more spectral understanding of gender, society is reordering itself and the resulting conversations can feel disarmingly chaotic. The expansion of the transgender umbrella to include as many gender non-conforming identities as possible means that you may look around the broad church you find yourself in and still feel somewhat cold. Historically, those of us who are not cisgender or heterosexual have tended to face more obstacles in finding love, intimacy, belonging and community. So it has often felt like we need to rely on each other. You deserve to find people who you relate to, who share your experiences and know what it feels like to be you.

Becoming your best self

The pursuit for peace with your gender identity may lead you to ask yourself questions that only you can answer. Mindfulness and meditation are invaluable tools that can help you listen to your own truth and deepen your conversation with yourself. We are living in a time where we have the freedom to be honest about our needs and desires. You can reach inside of yourself and manifest your essence – your true self.

It is essential that you become your own best friend. Protect yourself. Look after yourself. Defend yourself. Most of all, celebrate and enjoy yourself. You must believe that you are worthy of the joy that comes from being your best self.

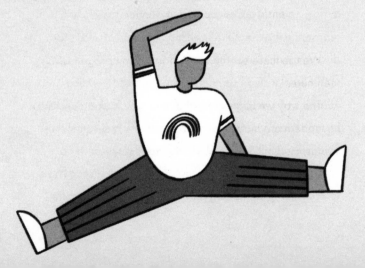

Transitioning

Historically, trans people around the world have had coming of age rituals that are seen as a reintroduction of themselves to the world or an evolution of their truest self. This may involve physical alterations, social (re)naming or an adoption of new spiritual practice.

The Lango people of Uganda had social practices for integrating trans people into their society through gendered renaming and adoption of tasks associated with their gender role.

In Haiti, Romaine-la-Prophétesse spoke of being possessed by a feminine spirit and commanded an uprising that was part of the Haitian Revolution between 1971–72 that caused the most noted self-liberation of enslaved Africans in the Americas.

We use these examples as proof that we have always been here.

The way we might conceive of gender transition in the modern era may be viewed as having three elemental strands: medical, social and spiritual transition.

Medical transition: Doctor Magnus Hirschfeld pioneered work at the Institute of Sexology in Berlin during the Weimar era (the interwar period where a more socially and politically liberal society in Germany flourished). His research indicated that sex hormone therapy and gender affirming surgeries were effective and assuaging methods for the alleviation of gender dysphoria in transgender patients. The process of self-identifying as transgender and seeking medical assistance with feeling comfortable in your body and using this pathway to gain legitimacy in society with name changes and differently gendered documentation really began here. Over the course of the twentieth century, Western medicine used such methods in their health systems and those with knowledge and access were able to jump through the necessary hoops to gain the medical assistance that saved many lives. Today, as well as hormone therapy, one may seek top surgery, bottom surgery, facial masculinization or feminization surgery and various laser hair removal or epilation procedures.

Social transition: many trans people change their names when they transition, although this is not essential. Whereas medical transition is to establish comfort in your body, social transition is to establish comfort in the world.

Perhaps changing your documentation and having the appropriate gender listed in personal identity papers will bring you greater ease moving through day-to-day life and relief that your sense of self corresponds with how you are spoken to and considered in society.

Spiritual transition: the inimitable Laverne Cox, American actor and LGBTQ+ advocate, speaks of her gender transition as a manifestation of the divine feminine. This means that in a sense one may have a spiritual sense of your feminine self. That there is a feminine goddess-like energy that is demanding to burst out of you and in so doing you will nourish the world with your feminine essence.

For Laverne Cox, the feminine spirit that resides inside of her required her to take the self-loving steps to express her femininity in a purposeful, glamorous and beautiful way in day-to-day life.

The supreme Angelica Ross, actor and businesswoman, whose incredible work has helped trans people in the tech industry, speaks of her Nichiren Buddhism practice being fundamental in her acceptance of herself and the manifestation of her highest self. This practice involves intense rituals of prayer and recanting mantras passed down through the centuries. Feeling the vibrations of one's voice saying these meaningful prayers cleanses the mind and spirit.

Whether religious, agnostic or atheist, the dictum that we are all spiritual beings having a human experience is a thoroughly inclusive statement that applies to us all. The metaphysical and philosophical implications of people dismissing their sexual assignment at birth will continue to ripple into the future and cause major change for those who are yet to inhabit the earth. Trans people have the power to transform our world as well as ourselves.

Be true to you

We might not be there to hold your hand as you continue on your own journey of self-discovery, but we want you to know that you're never alone. Here we have some wonderful advice from our friends and LGBTQ+ family to inspire and support you.

Jamie Windust, Author, Model and Editor
(they/them)

A bit of advice you say? Well ... one thing you must remember is that your story, your identity, your experience and your brilliance is yours to make. It's yours to create. Letting people into that story, that experience is a privilege because you're inviting them in to learn about the wonderful human being you are! So, if they don't understand straight away or are a bit confused, that's OK. Whether it be who you are, or who you fancy, they're all lovely little puzzle pieces that make up you, and you deserve to have those fit together in harmony. Remember there's always a fellowship of people out there that you can call family. Always. You're a superstar, and there's no time limit on how long it takes you to learn that. Every day you will learn just how much of a superstar you are.

Rhyannon Styles, Author and *Elle* Columnist
(she/her)

Listen to your intuition.

Chloe Filani, Poet and Artist
(she/her)

Focus on your transition and the person you may want to be. Don't beat yourself up for not always being on top of your transition, find ways to treat yourself and give yourself little joys. Find trans elders to look up to, even if it's just someone online. Remember, in your lows you don't have to be happy with your body, but be in love with your body that helps you breathe, see and be.

Francesca Martin, Model
(she/her)

My advice to my younger self at the start of my transition or to anyone reading this at the start of theirs would be to focus on loving yourself, because you're gonna face a lot of hate, but you'll be able to cope with it if you have a good foundation of self-love — it doesn't matter if the whole world hates you (and it might feel like that at times) if you truly love yourself. So much of our transition is focused around the work we get done externally but it's so important to remember that it's the inside work that matters most.

Xandice, Co-founder of Gal Pals (galpals.club) (they/them)

You're the only person who knows how you feel — trust your instincts and be gracious with yourself as you figure things out cos you don't have to have all the answers straight away. You're human and the best thing about us is our capacity for change.

Fox Fisher, Artist, Author and Film-maker (they/he)

I think it's hard enough being a teenager, let alone having to deal with gender issues. It's important to feel safe enough to explore your gender. Be kind to yourself. It's a game of patience. Focus on the things you can change and try to put the other worries to rest. Nothing can happen overnight; find something every day which you can do for yourself, so that it adds up over time. Find your tribe. Choose quality friends over toxic ones. It's OK to try things on, such as names, pronouns or clothing. Gender can be fluid. Life is a zig-zag so don't be focused on an end result — because transition never ends. What is important is your own happiness, right here, right now in the present moment. Ultimately the greatest gift you have for this world is to be yourself. You are important and you deserve to be loved and celebrated. Never settle for anything less.

The T

Charlie: Well, as our little chapter comes to an end, I hope it helped you! If you're cis, I hope it helped you to understand the basics a bit better. If you're trans I hope it helped you to understand *yourself* a bit better so you're ready to deal with the basic bitches when they come for you, which they no doubt will — but you are made from strong stuff. You come from a long line of strong trans people and you have this book and your big sisters, Kuchenga and I, to support you. You got this, baby!

Kuchenga: I am super grateful that we have been given this opportunity to share some of our thoughts with you. The process of putting this together has reminded me of how much I depended on Charlie to mirror some of my experience and I can only wish that you get the same support and love in your lives that we have been able to share with each other. I would never have made it through alone and there is no need for you to be alone either.

The process of writing this for you all has reminded me of how much I long to tell stories and share my experiences. It's the way I love to connect with the communities I belong to. I look forward to reading the stories you want to share. Our lives are important and I hope you will join me in celebrating our shared legacies.

coming out

There are so many differences between us — not just in terms of how we identify or who we love — but also the fact that we believe in different things, vote for different parties, support different teams, stan different pop divas and love or hate different foods, TV shows and books. Despite what the label "the LGBTQ+ community" implies, there is no one way of thinking that unites us, no single set of rules that all queers adhere to. We're all (brilliantly) quite different. That said, there is one unique experience that, at some point, we all consider and most of us will go through. Chances are you might be approaching it.

At some point in our lives, every queer person has to decide whether to tell the people around them about their innermost thoughts and feelings. That could be sharing that they are attracted to someone of the same gender or revealing their true gender identity. Unsurprisingly, sharing something so deeply personal is a big deal. It is the moment where you are essentially saying that you don't fit into the world's automatic assumption of cisgendered heterosexuality ... that you are "other". This is coming out.

Deciding whether to come out and be open and honest about our feelings, attractions, sexuality or true gender identity can be daunting, and it's a big step for a lot of people, so let's talk about it.

The one thing that I've learned from my own coming out experience and talking to others is that there is no right or wrong way to do it. (Remember what I was saying about us all being different?) So what can a chapter about coming out actually tell you? Well, I want you to hear some stories from other queer people about how they did it and then we'll look at some tips to make this a positive experience for you – because what is most important in all this is putting yourself first.

Before we dive into the details, here is a trinity of truth bombs that I want you to keep in mind.

1. You never stop coming out

It is not a "one and done" sort of experience where you never have to explain or correct someone again. Even now, having been out for over a decade, I still have some social situations or workplace interactions where I still have to come out. I tell you this now to help you set your expectations. Coming out never goes away but it does get easier. Sometimes you can even have a little fun with it.

2. Coming out actually means letting people in

Instead of seeing it as revealing a deep secret about you, see it as a gift that you are choosing to share with special and privileged people who you have allowed into your life in a more honest and authentic way. By sharing this part of yourself with others you are welcoming them and giving them a chance to get to know you and love you for your entirety. Coming out can be an act of love.

3. You are the priority in this process

This is one of those rare and precious moments where it is absolutely OK to focus on and prioritize what is best for you. Don't be uncaring about other people's emotions, but make sure you put your own comfort, happiness and safety first. You only have to come out when you feel ready and safe. If others react badly when you tell them, that's on them, not you. You do not have to hold on to or take ownership of anybody else's projected issues or concerns. You are fabulous just as you are.

Years of queers

The full phrase is "coming out of the closet" – but how did we end up with that expression? It's believed that the phrase "coming out" originated from Victorian high society, where debutantes (daughters of rich families) would "come out" from their "closeted" family homes (an old-fashioned phrase meaning secluded or sheltered) and be presented to society as eligible young women. This got mimicked and picked up and used by queer people coming out to other queer people as they entered into "gay society" – in queer spaces, such as Victorian molly houses (the Victorian name for meeting places for queer people) and later at drag balls in the New York queer scene. Some believe that the addition "out of the closet" came to popularity around the 1960s to signify the step taken out from a place of hiding. Just as we hide things from sight in cupboards, we hide away the queer parts of ourselves until we're ready to display them. And when we do display them, and "step out", the party begins.

Do I have to come out?

You shouldn't be pressured by anyone to come out —
not even by a secret girlfriend or boyfriend. If you aren't
ready yet, that is OK. This is your journey, in your own
time, so don't feel pressured or rushed. We all come to it at
different times.

There are people who make a choice to not come out
and to live their lives in secret and hide away from others.
And while it's not the choice that was right for me, they're
making the decision that they feel is best for them in their
lives at that time, as is their right. This decision to not come
out could be made for a huge number of reasons, such as
safety, cultural and religious upbringing, shame or even
living in countries with queerphobic laws. Together, as a
community, we face the choice repeatedly and often. And
yes, sometimes we make the decision not to — whether that's
for ease when we're tired of explaining ourselves to others or
for our safety when we're in a situation we're unsure about.

I won't do you a nasty by lying to you and pretending
that coming out is always easy or that it always goes well.
Sometimes it doesn't go the way we hope, and that is OK
— hard to handle, but still OK. Similarly, it's normal to be
worried, anxious or fearful. We'll look at how to helpfully
deal with those emotions in a little bit, but feeling these
nerves doesn't mean anything negative — you're not weak,
or anything like that. These emotions are something you
may feel, but they are not who you are.

A rainbow of emotions

You might decide that the time is right for you and you do want to come out. There are some amazing benefits to it. Coming out can make you feel:

yourself

relieved

softer

lucky

alive

free

joyous

strong

loved

liberated

confident

effervescent

powerful

authentic

lighter

honest

whole

complete

valid

real

taller

excited

empowered

elated

emancipated

connected

77

It will be OK. Why? Because you have no blame to carry here, you have not done or said anything wrong, you are not wrong. You are part of a line of people going back thousands of years of queers. You belong to a community and culture that has shaped art, science, history, pop culture, language, fashion and sport for thousands of years – and you are going to be OK. Better than OK, actually. You're going to be great and learn how to embrace yourself and shine all the more powerfully for it, and we can't wait to welcome you to the family.

What's it like when you come out?

We come out to many different people in many different places. Every situation is unique and you will need to appraise each one slightly differently – coming out to people you've known for a long time and care about deeply is different to coming out to people you've just met on your new Saturday job. Even coming out to family members can vary from person to person – age and expectations can make coming out to a sibling feel different to a parent and even more different to coming out to a grandparent. Likewise, coming out to each of your friends is its own experience, which can be different to coming out to teammates or teachers. As you may have picked up, it's always different, but while it is different each time, it ends up OK.

I'm coming out

Now we'll hear some stories from great people about the different ways they came out to their friends and families.

Jason Kwan, Singer-songwriter
(he/they)

Coming out was difficult. Growing up in Hong Kong, I did not know any other queer people so did not have any reference as to what coming out meant for me. My coming out was motivated by me wanting to be more honest with my parents about who I am. The conversations were tough and heart-breaking, but luckily it started a journey of acceptance for me and them.

Chris Bryant

Don't compare your personal experience with coming out to your queer friends. Sometimes, to protect your financial, emotional and physical well-being, coming out may not be an option. And that's OK! Your life doesn't need to look like anyone else's, and no one else can judge you for making decisions that impact your safety. If you are not in a place where you feel safe or supported by the people around you to come out, don't feel pressured to do so. Take your time building a better safety net of financial and emotional support before making a life-changing decision. There's no time limit and your mental and physical health should always come first.

Teddy Edwards

I didn't have a big conversation, I just brought a girl home one day and acted like it was entirely normal. I asked my mum more recently how she knew I was gay and she said that "having posters of naked girls all over my walls kind of gave it away."

Shane ShayShay Konno, Writer, Director and Founder of @bittenpeachuk (they/them)

I created a detailed plan for coming out, including an ordered list of who I would come out to and when. Coincidentally, both of my parents, without conferring with each other, brought it up with me before their allotted time on my coming out time plan.

Marc Thompson

I was lucky when I came out. Firstly, I told my head of year, who was supportive and gave me the contact details for what was then Gay Switchboard and some local gay youth groups. I also told my two best friends at my all-boys school in south London. They both surprised me with their "so what, big deal" response. I'm for ever grateful to them for that.

Yasmin Benoit, Model, Activist and Writer (she/her)

One of the most draining things about being asexual is other people's opinions about it. Don't be afraid to drown them out. You don't owe anyone an explanation and they don't know more about your sexuality than you do. Don't feel like you need them to understand to feel validated. Being content with yourself is the most important thing.

Looking after you: staying grounded

The pressures, thoughts and fears about coming out can be a lot and can feel overwhelming sometimes. Here is one of my favourite grounding techniques, designed to help you feel more in your body, less overwhelmed by your emotions and put you in the best emotional and mental space to tackle what's ahead – it's great for when you're feeling overwhelmed, nervous or anxious.

The 54321 method

We're going to ask ourselves five simple questions and really take our time to focus on the answers.

- Looking around you, name **five** things that you can see. Notice something about each of the objects, for example, their colour or shape – "a blue cup" or "a round vase".

- Focusing on your body, what are **four** things that you can physically touch? What do they feel like? A soft jumper? Some warm socks? A cosy blanket? A cool stone?

- Next, listening to the world around you. What are **three** things that you can hear? Pay attention to the rhythms and tempo – is there bird song around? How about the sounds of music or TV coming from somewhere? Are there any voices talking or the background hum of a washing machine?

- How about taste and smell — what are **two** things that you can either smell or taste? Is there a lingering perfume or the smell of washing powder? How about the taste of chocolate? Pay attention and see what you can tune into.
- Finally – and this is really important – what is **one** GREAT thing about you? Are you kind? Considerate? Hard-working? Trustworthy?

One of the great things about the 54321 method is that because it doesn't need you to do anything other than focus your mind, you can practise it anywhere – even in the classroom – and no one will know!

The right time to come out

Thinking and anticipating the "perfect time" to come out can add a lot of stress to the event, particularly when the Internet is filled with stories about teens who came out in big, filmic and dramatic ways — like announcing their gender identity to their entire school in their assembly speech, or turning up to a school dance surprising everyone with a beautiful same-gender date. Hats off to those people (if those experiences are true), but don't feel any pressure to measure yourself by those standards. For a lot of us, it starts in much quieter ways.

There is no rush to tell everybody or to have it all figured out immediately. Human identity and sexuality are incredibly complex and part of the joy of being human is continual growth and development — so take your time to explore

your identity and figure some things out for yourself. Not rushing out of the closet is not being fake or inauthentic, it can be an act of self-discovery that, in turn, is an act of self-love.

Some people like to wait for different "life events", such as starting a new school (or the break of summer holiday) or moving to university. Others meet a partner and want to share that as part of their new relationship. For some, it might be in response to a news item, a milestone birthday or seeing a positive portrayal of queer characters on TV. Everyone has their reasons, but that's the point — it's *their* reason. The most important question to ask yourself is "When is the right time for me?"

When I first told a friend, the only words I could get out were, "I think I like boys." The G-word stuck in my throat because I had never said "I'm gay" aloud to myself. Gradually, I evolved and grew more confident with myself, my identity and what my sexuality meant to me, and my confidence with my words followed. Crucially, though, this process has evolved over years and I've lost track of the number of times I've had to come out — to friends, family, university classmates, teammates, colleagues, employers. If that feels daunting, don't stress or lose heart. It is personal to us all. Trust yourself and your instinct to know what's right for you in each situation. And that first time I told someone, the "I think I like boys" moment, what was my friend's reaction? Honestly, I can't even remember. I can only remember the nerves I felt before and the relief I felt after.

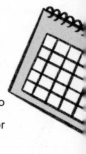

The "Oh no!" moment

Sometimes things don't go to plan and your coming out chat may not happen in quite the way you anticipated. Sometimes, private messages get read; sometimes, the pressure of rumour can build up. Sadly, I was outed at school before I was fully ready to "go public" (a friend I'd confided in had gossiped) and you'd be shocked at how common it is for an awkward family dinner discussion to come up about who's been watching gay porn on the computer. While these situations can be gut-wrenchingly horrible and not something anybody should have to go through, by following the same principles of prioritizing yourself, your own feelings and not thinking that you have to apologize or give any more explanation than you're comfortable with, you can protect yourself.

Staying true to you

Coming out can also be impacted by how we look. Some people are out by way of their visual representation, while others have what is known as "straight passing privilege". This is a thoroughly problematic notion that suggests we can simply look at somebody and know their sexuality. Usually, this kind of thinking is rooted in deeply sexist ideas of what men and women should look like and how they should behave. Sure, sometimes it is right, but sexuality and gender expression are fluid, personal things that appear in a myriad of ways. The important thing is not to worry about how you match up with an outdated perception of how masculinity or femininity should look and act, and do whatever is right, natural and comfortable for you.

Sometimes, when we come out, we'll hear "Ooh, I never would have known!" and have to handle that sticky and icky mix of pride and guilt – "Ooh, they wouldn't have known I was gay! WAIT – why am I pleased with that?" But that little voice (the voice of shame) is within all of us. Societal homophobia has infected us all, so this reaction doesn't make you a traitor, self-loathing or "a bad queer". It's understandable but don't worry, we'll discuss how to fight these bad feelings more in chapter seven, 'happy and gay'.

Time to open the closet

So, how do you go about coming out? Do you crack the closet door open a little bit and step a foot out, or do you throw those doors wide open and leap out? How you do it is entirely up to you. To help with your thinking, here is a rough guide to some things to think about and consider. Consideration is key, this is not a "how to" — personalize these points for you and your life because you are the expert on you.

Deciding who to tell: do you start with the most important people in your life, or do you start small and work your way up? Whoever it is, it should be somebody that you trust and you feel will treat your news with respect (and not as gossip). If somebody is upset that you didn't tell them first, that's not your issue and don't let this now become about them — you will tell people as and when it is right for you, and the order in which you tell people has very little to do with how you value them.

The when and where: when and where we're told something can have a surprisingly large impact on how we take in and process information, so it's helpful to give yourself the best chance of success by thinking ahead to the sorts of situation that might be most helpful. I had some great coming out discussions with friends one-to-one where we could really talk. Contrast this with an awful coming out on the spur of the moment to a friend at a loud house party where we had no privacy. Ask yourself, do you have space and time to speak openly and candidly, or might you be overheard, interrupted or rushed? Importantly, are you safe? If you're coming out to a friend on a night out, can you get home safely? If you are coming out to your family and are concerned about their reaction, have you considered your safety and – in rare cases – thought of an exit plan? It is important to remember, though, that these cases are rare and society's attitude towards same-sex attraction, gender identity and all things queer is improving and you'll most likely be OK.

Rehearsing your lines: having a run-through of your words can be helpful. A number of people I know – myself included – found ourselves "practising" by coming out online as anonymous profiles, talking over social media with other LGBTQ+ people in our position. Remember to be mindful of what you share online and keep your privacy protected.

Don't feel pressured to conform to labels: some of us know relatively quickly that we're lesbian, gay, pansexual or bisexual, trans or non-binary. Many people don't. Sometimes, ditching an identity word and saying "I like..." or "I fancy..." can be a softer, easier way into the conversation. Be clear on what you want to say and what information you're comfortable sharing and don't stray beyond that.

Boundaries: having clear boundaries around the conversation — and keeping to them — will help you feel much more comfortable because it's a way of keeping you in control. You do not have to give away more information than you feel comfortable sharing — whether this is what type of person you're interested in or even what label you use (remember, you don't *have* to use a label to describe your sexuality). Do not feel pressured to say anything, or answer anything, that you have not yet figured out for yourself.

The second boundary that I want you to set yourself is in terms of the response you get. Coming out to someone is gifting them with privileged access to the authentic you. If they react badly that is not your fault. Set a clear boundary of what you will and won't accept. It's important to understand that other people may need some time to process the news, but it's equally important to not accept any of their negative emotions — you are whole, perfect and special, being LGBTQ+ does not change that (if anything, it polishes it up and makes it shine all the brighter). Never apologize for being honest, being brave and being yourself, and do not accept someone else's projection of their issues onto you.

Advice for allies

How do you respond when someone else comes out to you? Whether you are queer, or whether you are an ally, we'll start with some things to avoid, and then look at some more specific examples.

Speculating about someone's gender or sexual identity before they've told you if they are out? Don't. It's that simple. Just don't. Don't add the pressure of gossip onto them. Help to make an open and supportive environment for people to express themselves in their own time. Gossip increases anxiety.

The OhMyGodPleaseDontEverSayTheses

"Omg! My friend *insert name* is gay! I can set you up!" Well-meaning, but not really considerate. At this point, this is more about our sexuality rather than who we are, what we're interested in or looking for in a partner.

"I don't like dresses either." So you're telling someone who has just told you a deep truth about themselves that their identity and true gender is the same as you not liking wearing dresses? No, not the same. Being trans isn't what you wear, it's who you are — no matter how many times I dress up as Wonder Woman, sadly it doesn't make me her.

"I love gay people." It's a nice thing to say, right? Well, eh, not really. It strips us of individuality and lumps everyone into a big blob. What they need right now is your love for them as their friend on an individual level.

"I've always wanted a gay best friend!" A girl that I went to university with genuinely yelled this cliché when I (quietly) came out to her during freshers' week, and it made the moment super uncomfortable. What this response does is to take your friend's coming out as part of your story and now makes it about you, falling into the "gay best friend" trope – where LGBTQ+ people are the supporting cast in films, TV and even life.

"Do you fancy me?" or **"You don't fancy me, do you?"** As I once got asked after telling a straight guy I was friends with (which, you know, made me feel really safe and secure – not!) This is taking someone else's narrative and making it about you. Plus, no. As heterosexuals are not attracted to everyone who is a different gender, we are not attracted to everyone of the same gender.

"Do you think I'd make a good woman?" Trans women aren't "making" at being women, they are women. Same for trans men. "Make a good woman" implies that their identity is all about how they look, which is not the case.

"I would never have known." or **"You can't tell."**
What are you aiming for here? Is it a reassurance? Is
it a compliment? Whatever the motivation behind this
phrase, it reinforces a belief (even subconsciously) that
heterosexuality is the desired norm. A norm they now
deviate from. Just don't say it.

"It's just a phase, you'll grow out of it." Do I need
to state this still? Apparently so. Just no. Don't.

"It doesn't matter." or **"I don't care."** OK, this one isn't
as bad as the others, it is much more well-meaning. What
could be wrong here? You're saying that their sexuality
doesn't matter to you? They've built up to tell you and a
response like this can feel dismissive and embarrassing.
Swap out this phrase for something like: "If you're happy,
I'm happy — that's all I care about." That makes it clear their
sexuality is not an issue for you in your relationship and
doesn't change how you think of them.

But what about when someone close to you comes out? Perhaps you've been surprised by someone's recent coming out and that's why you reached for this book or had it placed in your hands.

Understand: this is a process for them, they may have been living comfortably and proudly in their identity for a while and this rolls like water off a duck's back. Or they might not yet be as far down the yellow brick road. You should be able to ascertain this from how they tell you – did they seem nervous, was there a pause before, or was it an easily delivered piece of information? Think of the way they delivered the news, however big or small it seems to them, it should give you a direction as to where they are and to how you should respond. Try to match it appropriately. This understanding should extend to the fact that they might not have all of the answers yet, or they may have some mood swings (it can feel quite awkward and exposing).

Thank them: when someone comes out to you, they're telling you an important piece of information about themselves in the hope that you can get to know each other better. "Thank you for telling me," is a nice first response.

Reassurance: the level of reassurance that they need from you will obviously vary according to how they deliver it and how important your relationship is. If they have clearly struggled to tell you, they will need more reassurance that this doesn't change how you think of them and more importantly how you feel towards them — they are still your friend or family.

Let them lead: "Do you want to talk about it?" Let them decide how big this conversation is going to be right now. They might be exhausted from the build-up and anticipation of telling you, they might be fine and want to continue the discussion (and relieved that you've made it clear you're happy to talk about it) or they might not even need to talk about it.

Ask who else knows: you may be the first one that they have told, you may be halfway through, or you could be the very last person. Don't be offended about not being the first to be told (again, it's not about you).

Don't steal their story: taking somebody else's decision to come out to you and running with that information to tell everybody (without their permission) is not only a betrayal of the trust that they placed in you but can potentially put them in a difficult, awkward or unsafe situation.

Check in on them: a little while after they've told you their news, a little reminder that everything is OK, that you're happy for them and things can carry on as before – a text, a call, an email – can be wonderfully reassuring.

Respect their requests: if they have told you their new chosen name or pronouns, respect them and take the time to privately learn them. Similarly, if they have requested that you don't share their news with somebody else respect their requests.

Continue as normal: if you catch up every Tuesday morning and debrief on the new episode of your favourite show, meet to get a coffee every Sunday, head to the cinema to see whatever latest superhero franchise has been released, keep doing that and initiate the reminder that everything's fine – "see you Tuesday – I can't wait to see what happens", "Sunday morning, usual coffee place", "Can't wait for *Captain Non-Binary: Patriarchy Smash** on Wednesday". (*OK, probably not a superhero film coming out anytime soon.)

As an ally, whether you're a friend, parent or teacher – whoever – there's something that I want you to understand about our coming out experience. As queer people, we have to ask ourselves: "Is how they feel about me truly unconditional?" There is always a voice that says, "What if the answer is no?" That is a feeling we have to live with. It's not necessarily your fault, you could be the most accepting person and it would still creep in, but it is your responsibility to address it.

Paving your rainbow road

You've done it! You've stepped out of the closet. You're out! Congratulations! Well done! Hooray! Now what? Well, the reality is now that you have shared a part of your character with the world, you are more open to exploring what that part of your identity means to you and starting to claim your identity on your terms. Above all, enjoy your new freedom to explore yourself, discover yourself and love yourself.

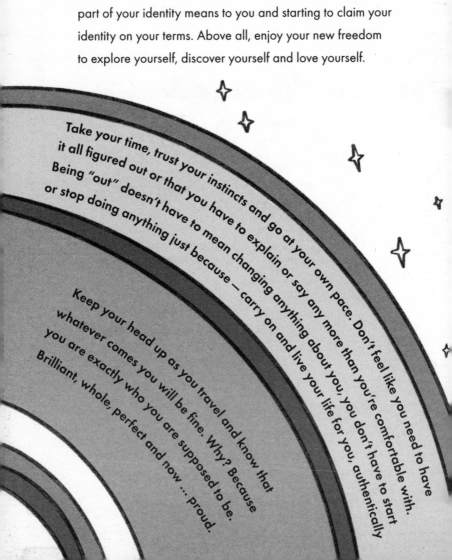

Take your time, trust your instincts and go at your own pace. Don't feel like you need to have it all figured out or that you have to explain or say any more than you're comfortable with. Being "out" doesn't have to mean changing anything about you, you don't have to start or stop doing anything just because — carry on and live your life for you, authentically

Keep your head up as you travel and know that whatever comes you will be fine. Why? Because you are exactly who you are supposed to be. Brilliant, whole, perfect and now ... proud.

families and friends

Families. They're strange things when you think about them, aren't they? We didn't ask to be part of them, they're often infuriatingly annoying, painfully embarrassing – like when my dad answered the phone telling the boy I had a crush on, "No, he can't come to the phone right now, he's having a poo, I think he'll be a while" – and we fight with them HARD. And then there comes the good stuff: the times they've cared for us, the love we feel, the support and kindness, the looking after us when we're sick, the comfortable understanding, the laughter. Nobody will challenge you more than your family, but nobody else will also help you grow and support you quite like them. But this is the thing – family is what we make of it.

The days of everyone having a mum and a dad, who have exactly 2.4 children (a weird statistic about the "average" family, which in my opinion does nothing but prove "normal" doesn't exist – what's 0.4 of a child?!) are long gone, if they ever existed in the first place, which I seriously doubt. A family can have a mum and a dad, sure, and multiple children. But families come in lots of different shapes and sizes, too. You can have just a mum, or just a dad. A child can be raised by their grandparents. They can be two halves of other families, separated and blended through divorce and marriage to form a unit of parents and step-parents and step-siblings. Alternatively, a family can be formed between one person and a best friend. It can be adopted, fostered or created in an unlimited number of ways.

Myself? I've actually got two dads — no, they're not together and never have been (ohgodpleasedontmakemeimaginethatgross). One is my biological father and the other is my step-dad, they both raised me, they both taught me life lessons and helped me grow into the person I am. Then there's my mum who, for the first years of my life raised me as a single parent — another valid and incredibly important family unit. Rounding it out, I have step-family too — step-mums, step-sisters and brothers, even step-nibblings (did you know 'nibbling' is the collective term for nieces and nephews? Pretty cool isn't it?) all of whom, to me, are my family that I love and care about.

Even a group of friends can be a family. The bonds and love for one another run deep and hold strong, stronger than so-called "familial ties", and bring them together. Many queer people have a "chosen family" or what legendary queer writer Armistead Maupin coined as "logical families" (get it? Like biological families except they're people that just *make sense* to you and your life). Many of my friends take an important place in my heart, life and in my logical family — they are as much family to me as anyone and far more so than some random distant second cousins!

Whatever shape our family takes, however they're made up, they're unique to us. They're important people, they're some of the most important people in our lives. But families can also be a complicated headache, especially when it comes to understanding, exploring and expressing our sexuality and gender identity. Though I will say the first and most important person in your life should be you. So, while we may feel great about our identity ... will they?

Remember, by telling your closest family and friends about your personal journey, you're giving them an opportunity to recognize and celebrate how you have grown, who you authentically are and to be there for you along the journey. You'll probably also inspire some growth and reflection in them too!

It's understandable to be nervous about these conversations (and don't forget, in the first chapter we looked at what to do if anxious thoughts get overwhelming). Working out how to tell your nearest and dearest is an important step, so let's look at how you can plan for this.

Family ties

The thought of speaking to your family about your sexuality or identity can feel overwhelming. But remember, you're also part of a big queer family and community, and here we have stories and messages of support to help you on your journey.

Kayza Rose

I was 24 and with my first woman partner, who was very out. She became frustrated by the fact that I wasn't claiming her as my partner when others were around; she gave me an ultimatum. I took this on as something you're expected to do if you were "really queer" and not just sleeping with women here and there. It's a kind of rule, you don't really have a choice — that's how I felt anyway. I went to my closest cousin first, he laughed and said he knew all along and was wondering when or if I'd ever come out. I always thought he was gay anyway so it seemed like the safest place at the time. He ended up outing me to another close relative, not so safe in the end, but hey.

I then went on to tell my father some fabricated story about a gay friend of mine and asked whether he'd still like or speak to this person knowing their sexual orientation. He said it wouldn't matter to him and that it's still the same person. That made me feel good about telling him so I jumped in with a follow-up, "What if the gay person was me?" He laughed and said it wasn't possible and tried to move the conversation on. I told him that it was true and that it is me. He couldn't quite grasp the fact that you can bear children in a heterosexual relationship and they can still be queer ... it went totally over his Jamaican head, bless him. He did manage to tell me that I'm his daughter and he loves me, that was comforting. He spent the next few years getting excited about any male friend I had, in the hopes that this was the one man who could "bring me back", LOL. He has come to accept who I am over time; he's had no choice.

My mother's reaction was more emotional, she wanted to know if anything had happened to make me feel this way. I assured her that this is just how I feel, but I felt like I was disappointing her. I've never doubted my mother's love, she's always been affectionate and never misses a chance to tell me she loves me. This never changed, she never treated me differently or shunned me.

I realize that the reaction from my parents is a massive privilege and also the fact that I live in the UK where there are laws and services to protect me and others who are same gender loving or on the LGBTQ+ spectrum. I probably wouldn't have felt so safe if I was in Jamaica or Cameroon (part of my cultural background). Interestingly, colonialism is the reason those two places are unsafe for us and yet the cause of this hateful behaviour has now outlawed it. I want us to hold space thinking about this.

Chris Bryant

My family is very conservative, so the process wasn't easy. I came out during the "It gets better" movement to my extended family, and I remember being bitter at all the televised spots about how amazing and easy coming out is. I feel like my mindset changed when I realized that coming out is a process. We have to come out to people every day, and our gender and sexual identities are always changing and evolving. There will be days when it is easy, and days when it's difficult — and that's OK.

Jason Kwan

Understanding who you are, and helping other people understand who you are, are going to be long journeys — but they will be worth it. It takes some people a lifetime to understand something, so give them and yourself the opportunity to learn.

Ryan Lanji

It was really hard because it was my mom who found out and asked me straight up. I couldn't bear to lie to her for peace and only break her heart again in the future, so I bit the metaphorical bullet. Our friendship changed drastically that day but fortunately eleven years later I know her love is still the same.

Elliot Douglas

My mum reacted badly to me coming out as bisexual at fourteen and then worse as a trans man at seventeen. It was really tough, especially as I was homeless for some time as she had kicked me out. A few years later, time has been a great healer and she is much better with it all now. I am happy she has more understanding today, but as a child and her being my parent, I needed her support and love in my life when I was coming out.

Stu Oakley, Film Publicist and Co-host of the podcast *Some Families* (he/him)

"Oh, I'll never have grandchildren", "I worry you will live a lonely life", "I just want you to have a family" are all decades-long stock responses from parents when their children come out. The notion that LGBTQ+ people can't have families is now hopefully dead in the water. Just like our straight friends not everyone wants to have children, but know that if you want a family you can have one. There are so many ways queer people can have children, from adoption to surrogacy to IUI/IVF or even co-parenting, that you can find a way that fits how you want to be a parent. You might not be at the stage to start digging into loads of research so for now just know that if you are dreaming it, it's possible.

Looking after you: how to have a N.I.C.E conversation

N.I.C.E is an acronym that I use to help me set up important conversations to help make sure that they are structured and healthy. It's a helpful way I remind myself to make sure I say what I want to say and communicate it clearly.

Needs – let the other person know what you need from this conversation, "Mum, Dad, I want to talk to you and I need you to listen until I'm finished, please. OK?"

Impact – share with them the impact this is having on you and how you're feeling, "I'm feeling pretty nervous right now because this is really important to me."

Consequences – help them understand why it's important for you to talk about your journey, "It's been weighing on my mind and not being able to talk to you about this has been really hard for me."

Expectations – set out why you're sharing this with them and what you'd like to come from it, "So I hope by sharing this with you we can be closer, you can understand me better and help me on this journey."

I'm not saying you have to follow that exact script – you are the expert on you and your family – I'm just giving you some pointers as to how to frame the conversation with people in your life to help them understand how important it is for you, how to make this conversation better for you and what you hope to get out of it. We love our family and friends, but we are the most important ones in this conversation so let's set it up for our best success. After all, when something feels quite big and daunting, making a plan for how we're going to tackle it is a great way to put ourselves back in control and challenge those fears.

Staying in control

We covered a lot of the nuts and bolts of "the conversation" when we discussed coming out together in the third chapter. There are a few added things to think about when it's our close family or friends.

Be specific on who they can or can't tell: are you a close group of four friends, but only telling one or two right now? Be clear that they are not to tell others, that's for you to do when you are ready. Similarly, if you are telling a sibling or a parent, tell them who they can or can't share this information with within your family.

Be positive: people who love us want the best for us. If we frame it in a way of us wanting to share with them because we want to be closer with them and that we're happy with who we are, that will help them feel more reassured.

Understand they may need time: from the moment we're born (often even before that) our parents are dreaming up what our futures may look like, making wishes and plans for our future – finding out that their child is queer might be a bit of a shock, not always because they have a problem with it but sometimes they need a moment to reframe their thoughts and change the story they've been telling themselves.

Reaffirm that this is for you and not about them: this being said, their hopes for your future and what they've imagined for you is not your responsibility, nor your burden to carry. We only have one life, so we have to live a life that we want, not a life that someone else has imagined for us.

Make a safety plan: fortunately, this is not needed for everyone. The majority of coming out conversations go well, but there is still a small percentage where conversations don't go as we deserve (and you really do deserve it to go well) and so we need support. If your parents have made queerphobic comments or remarks, it is understandable to approach this with more caution. Remember, you are under no pressure to come out before you are ready to – and part of being ready is protecting your safety.

Worries and bad reactions

Unfortunately, sometimes it doesn't go quite the way we deserve. Here is a look at some practical steps you can take to help you support yourself when difficulties arise and things don't go to plan with family and friends.

Managing Rejection

1. **Understand your feelings:** it's not that you're being overly sensitive or weak, it's that it matters. You've shared something important and personal and you've not had that care and love returned to you in the way that you deserve. We're left feeling hurt. Remember, you are OK and have done nothing wrong.

2. **Prioritize yourself:** take a step back, disengage from any negativity until the situation has settled to prioritize your own well-being and stability. If someone else behaves badly or says or does something inappropriate, you don't have to meet fire with fire. You can clearly defend your boundaries and refuse to accept being spoken to in ways you don't deserve.

BOUNDARY

3. **Rebuild:** check in with some people you know who have got your back and support you unreservedly. It's important to remind ourselves that we do have other people who are on our side. As part of this, do something that you're good at that you enjoy, it's a great way of reminding yourself that you are awesome.

4. **Love yourself:** this is a great time to practise some self-care and do some things that make you feel good. Take time to look after yourself because you are so special.

5. **Reach out to Shout:** you are never alone. For free, confidential support, text 'SHOUT' to 85258 and someone will be on hand to listen and talk with you.

For more information on places to go to for support, turn to the back of the book for the resources list.

Advice for allies

Family and friends have a big role to play in this journey. There is work to be done – and it's your job to do it. You can help make a worrying and difficult experience a lot easier by offering support and understanding. It's important to make sure that your child, or your friend, knows that you are happy and proud of them for taking a step further towards being who they are.

- Listen to your loved one and give them the time and space they need.
- Let them know your thoughts and feelings towards them have not changed.
- Understand – and I say this with the greatest respect – that this is not about you. This is not about your feelings, fears or what sort of future you'd imagined for them (and thereby yourself as you got older). This is about your child, or your friend, living their lives happily as themselves. We all know how stressful the burden of someone else's expectations can be. Free them from it.
- Love them. That's all you have to do. Love them and unreservedly accept them. That's it. Love them and all other things will come naturally with time.

The gay best friend

At some point, it's quite possibly going to happen to you. Someone is going to excitedly shriek "I HAVE *ALWAYS* WANTED A GAY FRIEND!" at you, becoming overly familiar, pouring out all sorts of jumbled catchphrases they learned from watching *Drag Race* or *Queer Eye*. It can be fun, at first, even a relief to feel like there's someone on your side who is celebrating you ... except ... it's not really what's happening. In their mind, you're this finger-snapping caricature that they can go shopping with, tell all their problems to and have console them through boy problems. The problem is ... it's always about them.

An actual ally, a true friend, will embrace your sexuality as part of you – not all of you – and see you for who you are, not what conveniently fits into their life. Because our sexuality is important, it's a wonderful part of us, but we're unique and special individuals who deserve to be seen as such. Don't let anyone push you into playing a role, just because it's what they want you to be.

Friends and chosen families

As important as they are, our families are not the only people in our lives. Our friendships, and the platonic relationships we build with new people in our lives, can be just as deep and meaningful. These chosen families have a special bond – my lezzie bezzie Jess is genuinely like a sister to me; my dear friend Dillon and I share a deep brotherly connection (without the fighting); I have an adopted 85-year-old gay grandad; two straight girlfriends, Ana and Abbie, who have always been understanding champions and allies; and even an ex who has become part of the family and is that slightly weird cousin you love anyway (Hi, Stinks!).

Don't fret if these magical people aren't around in your life just yet – these relationships take time to grow and form, and people this special are wonderful, rare diamonds that you'll gradually encounter as you grow and go through life. In all honesty, I'm not in touch with anybody from my school days – a random allocation into a class at school was not how I found the people I clicked with. I've made my logical family over time and through chance meetings as our lives have been brought together by shared interests, passions and adventure – not just because we happened to live in the same postcode at fourteen. Those are the rich friendships that will transform your life, and they're out there for you.

Chris Bryant

Being LGBTQ+ means that I have a family of people from all walks of life that I can connect with on a deep emotional level. It means I can create my own life and family based on the morals I find important, rather than by society's rules. I get to live outside of the box, I get to be free, and I get to redefine myself daily.

Finding your people

So how do we go about finding our tribe and our real friends and allies? As I mentioned, our sexuality and our gender identity can play a large part in who we are and how we navigate the world — but it's not *all* we are. Not every lesbian is going to be friends with every lesbian. Not every trans man is going to have stuff in common with every other trans man. And that's where queer interest groups can be transformational.

One of the things that I love the most about being LGBTQ+ is that whatever you're into, somewhere, there will be an LGBTQ+ group dedicated to that thing that you geek out about and love. From queer dance troupes, to sports teams, to music groups, book clubs, debate societies, art nights, poetry slams, board gaming, travel organizations ... there's something out there for you. You just have to get looking and with the Internet, it's never been easier. I'm sure you don't need me to tell you how great the Internet can be to help you connect with fans of stuff you're into, that can often be a good first step towards building your IRL logical family, by building an online support group.

(I'm gonna put on my big brother voice now — remember to stay safe when connecting with strangers online, in our chapter on love and dating there are some tips on this. I know you know this, but it's important to remind ourselves of these things sometimes.)

Welcome to the club!

One of the wonderful, special things about being queer is how it can be transformational and powerful for relationships and forging special bonds.

Elliot Douglas

Being a part of two marginalized communities meant growing up I felt lonely, I didn't know anyone like me personally, or see anyone like me in the media. However, I found myself in the queer community before I found myself in the deaf community and I always felt at home in the LGBTQ+ community and have always had a place here. My advice to young queer folk would be to try and attend your local LGBTQ+ group as this is where I began to find myself in my LGBTQ+ identity. When I was exploring my trans identity, it was at one of the weekly group meetings that I tried out different names and used my chosen name for the first time.

Ryan Lanji

You are home. You are your tribe. There are others like you. Go find them! EXPLORE! Friends might not stick around for ever and family can be a tricky word to use, but trust you'll meet the right souls along the way and the adventure will be worth it when retold for generations to come. Your tribe are your people who make you feel safe and seen, it takes time but when you find them it's SO WORTH IT!

Masuma Rahim

Support can come from different places. Find people you trust to confide in as you explore your identity and your sense of belonging. It's much harder to go it alone. The community is a complex and multifaceted thing. Not all parts of it will be for you, and that's fine. The key thing is to find your tribe, and it often takes time to do so. Keep your options open and explore a range of spaces, but make sure you keep yourself safe. It can be tempting to throw yourself in, but it's OK to take it slowly.

Marc Thompson

Sometimes it takes trial and error to find our communities and as we are never just "one thing" we will occupy multiple communities. I'd say test them out. If they don't meet your needs, then be brave and create the space yourself. My activism has been driven by the lack of space, virtual and real, that has been absent from our community, for Black and brown people.

Shane ShayShay Konno

I first figured out during puberty that I was full of homosexual attraction, and awaited the right time (for me) to come out as gay, assuming that all the unease I felt inside would be solved. But I still felt so out of place in the gay male scene. The thing setting me apart was my non-binary identity, which I didn't yet have the vocabulary to describe. It took attending gender-diverse queer events and meeting fellow trans people to give me the words and the confidence to come out as non-binary.

it must be love

One of the most confusing, socially stressful and awkward — and yet so important and *fun* parts of teen life — is dating. It's a whole minefield, navigating your own feelings, navigating the feelings of others and doing all of that for the first time with others watching and yet we keep doing it. There's heartbreak, there are some tears and sleepless nights, but God there is so much *joy* too. The butterflies, the will-we-won't-we moments, sheepishly returned smiles that speak a secret language, the joy when your hand brushes theirs and is held, the static crackle of your first kisses — such special and powerful moments are why we keep going back.

Dating is rarely easy for anyone — there's a cruel irony that our dating exploration tends to begin in our teens just as our hair gets greasy, our skin breaks out (I know from personal experience, dating with acne feels impossible sometimes), our bodies start to change, our emotions fly all over the place and our voices crack and wobble.

And let's be honest, being a queer teenager adds a whole other layer of confusion and trickiness to dating. It can often feel like we're alone and like there's nobody around there for "us", but your time will come. It's even more complicated when we factor in that we may not have come out yet to everyone around us (if at all) or that those we fancy may also not be fully open about their sexual identity. There's a high chance that they might not even understand it yet either. I can remember having secret make out sessions with a guy after school, kept hidden from everyone else.

During the day, we'd barely acknowledge one another, but in private ... well ... we couldn't keep our hands off each other.

Secret crushes and hidden romances are common for us queers. In some ways, they're great because they allow us to privately figure these things out for ourselves without other people prying their noses in or asking questions we haven't yet answered for ourselves (there are those questions again!) – but sometimes, unfortunately, secret romances can be unhealthy. What to look out for here is when you're in public: are they still treating you with respect? My secret school fling didn't acknowledge me in the classroom, but that was OK as we agreed upon that together. What wouldn't have been OK was if there had ever been anything disrespectful – for example, him siding with a bully who was saying something mean to me.

Mutual respect and care for one another has to be the foundation of any relationship you go into – whether that's out in the open or not, whether that's romantic or platonic. Be respectful of others, their hearts and feelings, and don't put up with others who would disrespect your own. Just as we deserve the right to explore and understand our identity, attractions and feelings in our own time, so too do others. Don't push anyone to come out (or feel pushed to come out), if what works best is keeping things quiet for you both, then do, but do so with respect, understanding and an agreement. At the end of this chapter, we look at healthy boundaries in relationships to give you some more info.

Looking after you: the worry tree

There can be a lot of worries wrapped up in dating – anxious, overbearing thoughts that can crowd out the good and fun feelings of this exciting step and can make us feel rubbish. When we have lots of worries filling our heads it can feel overwhelming and huge. How do we deal with that big dark cloud of thoughts? The simplest way is by taking all the different worrying thoughts that can fly around in our minds and chipping away at them one by one with the help of the worry tree. The worry tree is a simple way of looking at individual issues through a yes/no lens where we ask ourselves "can I do anything about that?"

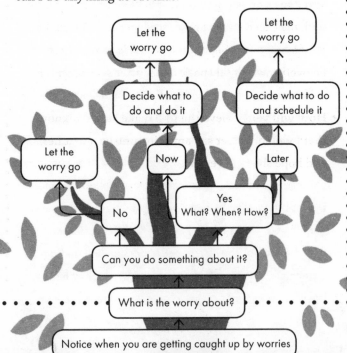

Let the worry go

Let the worry go

Decide what to do and do it

Decide what to do and schedule it

Let the worry go

Now

Later

No

Yes
What? When? How?

Can you do something about it?

What is the worry about?

Notice when you are getting caught up by worries

Here is an example of a worry that you might come across at home or in school.

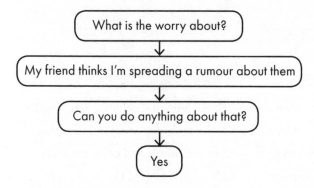

When you come to a "yes" make the action tangible and think: **what, when, how**.

- **What** are you going to do that will help? I'll speak with my friend so she knows this isn't coming from me.
- **When** are you going to do it? Class is too likely to be overheard, so I'll speak to her after school on the way home.
- **How** will you achieve this? I'll make sure she knows that I wouldn't ever say anything untrue about her, and hope she believes me.

Where are they?

OK, if everyone keeps saying "there'll be someone out there" then WHERE ARE THEY?! Right? It can feel quite lonely or like we're the only one without a girlfriend/boyfriend or a date. It's understandable that you might want to look around but it is a little tricky if you don't feel like you connect with some of the people at school. Because of this, it's increasingly common for people to meet online. Whether that's originally chatting as like-minded friends on a fan forum, bonding over your mutual fave, and then you realize there's maybe something more. Or even sometimes meeting people through real-world events organized online. Big, trustworthy organizations such as Young Stonewall and the Albert Kennedy Trust hold youth events and conferences for young queer people where you could meet and make friends IRL and maybe those could even spark something.

The most important thing is to remember that there really is no rush. If the only other queer teen you know isn't someone you have anything in common with, and the idea of kissing a bin is more appealing, don't force yourself to have feelings for them just because they're the only option currently present. You don't even like them! Waiting for the right person and the right time is absolutely fine.

Dating online

Dating apps are the most common way that LGBTQ+ people find dates and partners. But there's a snag: these are designed for people over eighteen and are often quite sexually focused. As tempting as it may be to make an account online or on an app, there are a few important reasons why you shouldn't:

- Those apps are designed for adults. There are very strict rules around inter-age dating and making an account with a fake date of birth and pretending you're over eighteen could be putting someone else at risk of accidentally breaking the law. These laws are there to protect you but you also have a responsibility to follow the rules as well so that you stay safe.

- Some people don't have the best intentions. It's a scary thought, but not everybody will abide by that principle of "don't be reckless with other people's hearts". Unfortunately, it can be pretty difficult at times to suss out who is genuinely well-meaning and who might be playing a game. You're smart but while you're young you are more vulnerable to people who are more predatory. Minimize your risk by not swimming in the murky waters of hook-up apps until you're older and have a bit more experience and street smarts under your belt to help keep you safe.

Social media

But if you can't find someone at school and you can't go on the apps, what can you do? Obviously, social media plays a huge part in dating life too (no points to me for stating the obvious there). There are also LGBTQ+ teen forums and message boards that you can use as a way of expanding your online network and finding confidantes and friends. Then, if there are one or two (or more) who you spark with, swap social media profiles when you're ready and get to know them better. Clearly, though, social media is not a perfect utopia where everything is wonderful, goofy filters and entertaining dances, so check out our top tips for staying safe online at the back of the book.

God, I feel so old saying this now, but one of the ways I met other queer teens (and met the guy that I went on my first ever boy-boy date with) was through an LGBTQ+ youth group. Yes, these quaint, old-fashioned things actually still exist and are dotted all around the country. Going for my first time, I was very nervous — what would the people be like? Would anyone talk to me? Would there be anyone I knew there? But it was super easy and relaxed. Sure my nerves made it a little awkward at first, but I quickly felt comfortable there, knowing I could just be myself and not worry about sexuality or whether I'd "give myself away". We just hung out, chatted and ate pizza. Eventually, I even had my first kiss at my youth group. Totally worth it.

Friends or more?

When you do eventually meet someone, there is sometimes this funny little back and forth we do in our heads, trying to work out if we like someone as a new friend or if we like, like them. Trust your gut and don't try to force yourself to feel something you don't. Not being into someone isn't always a bad thing – you've potentially just made a great new friend!

Advice for allies

How's this reading for you? I hope it's giving you a deeper understanding of how lonely it can sometimes feel being LGBTQ+ and why your friend might sometimes feel a bit remote or fed up as you talk about another date or relationship – because, for us, we don't often get as many options. It's not that we're being a bad friend when we lose our patience because you're talking about your relationship ... *again*. It's not actually about you, it's that we really want that for ourselves too. Most of the time, we'll manage to be happy for you, just be understanding if we don't always manage it. As we're on the topic of understanding – a big one for you is to be understanding, graceful and respectful if, or when, you're lucky enough to find someone of the same sex crushing on you. Thank them, let them know you're flattered but sadly you just don't feel that way. How you handle these moments really is the core of your allyship.

Holding hands and making plans

There are few things as exciting in life as those first moments of "... *are we going to?!*" Whether that's saying "hi", smiling at one another across a classroom, holding hands or sharing a first kiss. These are wonderful moments which are special, and you'll have many of them — so enjoy them as they come. Sometimes, a huge part of the enjoyment of crushes is the anticipation and imagination of what could be. Daydreams of what it would be like if you were together, mental plans of how to come up with the perfect thing to say. We can scrutinize every little moment and interaction for a sign that maybe they fancy us too.

One hurdle we have to awkwardly navigate through is sexualities. Everybody I know has had an unrequited crush on someone who, unfortunately, just isn't feeling the same-sex love. That's OK, it can't be helped — the important thing is you remember that it's not about you, nothing you say or do could change that. If the person you are crushing on doesn't return those feelings, accept it with grace and try to let those feelings go. Sure, have a cry about it, moan about it, have a sulk to help get it out of your system. It's hard and it's hurtful, but it's not their fault or yours.

Agony Aunt dating advice

They say that an expert is "someone who has made every conceivable mistake in a narrow field of endeavour"... and boy have I made some mistakes in my time. Absolute howlers, in fact. I cringe when I think of the time I started to make out with a guy and sneezed all over him! Those big, stringy globs of snot and all. In my defence, it was summer and I have bad hay fever, but that poor guy. (Tom, if you read this, I'm so sorry.) With that in mind, let me now share with you some dating advice from me and some other tips that have been learned from our embarrassing failures and mistakes, so that you don't have to do the same.

How to tell if someone likes you back:

The obvious thing is to ask but that can feel terrifying. Look for signs of returned smiles, held eye contact, laughter, them remembering things you talk about and moving slightly closer to you. With time, it'll grow to be something that you can "feel".

When is the "right" time to date?

Honestly, that is entirely up to you. Some people keep their heads down and focus on performing well in school, relieved to not get caught up in the petty dramas of who's dating who so they can do well and go off to uni. Others throw themselves into it and can think of nothing more important than finding someone to date.

Whatever is right for you, know that most LGBTQ+ people come to dating slightly later (due to our lack of proximity to other queer teens) – so you're not alone or weird.

Meeting someone for the first time: If you do meet someone online and want to meet them for real, then you should still plan for your safety, even if you're confident that they are who they say they are (you've seen them on video, for instance). Tell somebody who you're meeting, when and where you're meeting them and make sure that the "where" is a safe public place – like a coffee shop – with plenty of other people about. If you have a friend who you're out to and trust, ask them to accompany you to the coffee shop and then sit in the background like your secret agent backup (secret disguise optional but encouraged for the drama).

Bad dates will happen: Whether there was just no chemistry, or something embarrassing happened, it can feel mortifying in the moment, but that embarrassment will pass. One day, you'll look back at it and laugh. I promise.

Engaging, meeting people and building new friendships is an important part of learning how to date. **Get out there:**

You will fancy a straight person:

It happens. It's a reality. We can fancy or fall for people who don't share our same-gender attraction. That's OK — just as we can't be "changed" by others to be straight, we can't change others to be queer. Let the crush pass, there's nothing else you can do.

Nobody likes to feel ditched. When you do start seeing someone, as tempting as it can be to spend all your time with them, don't forget your friends. Your friends will be the ones who are there for the break-up, which inevitably will happen because...

Remember your friends:

Break-ups do happen:

They can feel rubbish. Utterly heart-breaking. But keep your head — you can't control what someone else does, only what you do and how you respond. Take the high road, take time and take space. Don't lash out, don't be cruel and certainly never out someone as revenge, share their secrets or say bad things about them. That only disrespects the good thing you once shared. Oh yeah, and don't immediately make out with or start dating one of their friends (sorry, Tony!). That's not fair on anybody in the equation.

Prioritize yourself: When you do start dating, don't lose yourself. You are your own longest relationship so don't compromise your own well-being, comfort and enjoyment for someone else.

Don't lose your head: In an age where we have read receipts on so many of our forms of communications it can be agonizing when you know your message has been read but that they haven't yet replied. Remember, those blue ticks or the "seen" status only tells you that the message has come up on their phone screen. It doesn't tell you if they're busy doing homework or chores, whether they're free to reply or if they saw it but their battery died, so trust that they'll reply when there is time.

Trust: It's a big one but you have to place trust in the people you date. Trust that they'll reply when they can, trust what they're saying to you. Don't try and check their phone or social media. If someone is untrustworthy, you'll feel it in your gut. If you don't have trust in your relationship — (not) sorry to break it to you — you don't really have a relationship.

Be yourself: It can make dating an absolute headache if we go in trying to change ourselves or pretend that we're someone else. Changing how we talk, what we talk about, how we dress, what we say we're into and so on — it's tempting, but it's exhausting and ultimately doomed. The right person for you will fall for you, not someone you're pretending to be.

Handle rejection well: We won't be liked back by everyone so rejection is inevitable. Take it well, with grace, a smile and a "that's a shame, but no problem" (even if you're hurting inside). Your crush will pass, the embarrassment and pain of rejection will also fade — don't be cruel or try to reject them in return. That only prolongs the bad feelings.

And remember, if you have hay fever for God's sake take an antihistamine before going in for a snog.

Love knows no bounds, but it should know boundaries

As someone who has had my own fair share of dates and relationships and who also works with sex and relationship therapy, one of the key bits of advice I can give you to setting up your relationships to not only succeed and be lovely but also to be nourishing and safe for you is to establish your boundaries together.

Boundaries and shared understandings are essential so that we can make one another feel secure, supported and respected – vital building blocks for love and relationships. Setting some of these out from the start helps you get better at saying what you need. My top tips:

Happy talk: Be clear about what kind of talking and communication works for you – how you like to talk, how frequently, etc. For example, I am positively allergic to phone calls but I will happily talk on video for aaaaages. If I just say no or make an excuse to my partner when they want a phone call, that won't feel nice for them. But if I explain that "I actually prefer a video call, it means I get to see you, and I feel like we understand each other better when I can see you too – plus, I like looking at your face," that's a positive way of framing it, as opposed to "no, I don't like talking on the phone." For me, I don't need them to comment on everything I post on social media, that's not important to me, but what is important to me is to say good morning and goodnight to the person I'm dating. It doesn't have to be big, just a quick "morning x" or "night, handsome x". It means a lot to me — so I explain that upfront. Help your communication go well by talking about how you like to communicate and what you need.

Clear commitment: Once you've got clear communication, I fully encourage you to then go for clear commitment. Be upfront about what sort and types of commitment you want from your partner and what is or isn't OK. This is not about controlling your partner but explaining what sort of things could lead to accidental hurt. For example, I have no issue at all with my partner being in contact with his ex (I actually think it's a positive thing, it means they managed a healthy and respectful ending, which only says good things) but the commitment I ask him to make is that he let me know. Similarly, we should be clear about what we're entering into — are we dating multiple people, exclusively dating, or in a relationship? Have these chats so you know where you stand. Sometimes, it can feel scary to have this discussion because what if they don't want the same commitment? Well, I hate to break it to you, but you didn't have it anyway and not speaking about it wasn't going to get you it. It's best you find out quickly and avoid getting deeper into the feels.

Boundaries in space: I was raised as an only child so I need a lot of alone time. For an ex of mine (who was one of four), this was the total opposite of what he needed. Because we hadn't communicated our needs for personal space, it became a source of conflict. Being clear about if/when/how you need personal space can save a lot of those agonizing: "Why haven't I heard from them?", "Are they mad at me?" thought trains. We understand that no, they're not annoyed at us, they just need some alone time because that's how they recharge. It's not a negative reflection on me or our relationship.

Physical and sexual boundaries are a MUST in all relationships. Nobody else has a given right to your body, even when we are in a relationship, but physical intimacies and boundaries around sex are more than just a point in a list — so let's get into it in full in the next chapter.

Physical intimacy and boundaries:

let's talk about "it"

As teen hormones go into overdrive and S-E-X starts to raise its head (no pun intended), it can sometimes feel like it's all that matters. And it does matter, but only as much as you decide it matters to you, whenever you're ready to make anything of it. That being said, the legal age of consent in the UK is sixteen — in the eyes of the law, you are not ready before then.

Our society is obsessed with sex. Like properly obsessed. It's in nearly every song. Adverts sell us things by making their products seem sexy. Films often carry some steamy subplot. Entire programmes that are dedicated to watching people shagging are now prime-time TV shows. And yet, weirdly, as out there as it is, we rarely actually talk about it properly. Strange paradox, isn't it?

Understandably, sex is a tricky conversation topic. We can get caught up in the awkwardness and the embarrassment of it — I can remember screaming from the cringe as my mum tried to talk to me about sex. But she quickly put me in my place with the words, "If you're not mature enough to talk about sex, then you're not mature enough to have sex." And wow, she was right.

She was right because sex can be a big deal. In fact, all forms of intimate and sexual activities, from holding hands to making out and more can feel like A LOT. It's important to take it at your own pace, think it through and really make up your mind about what feels right for you. You are the expert on you. You are the only person in charge of your body. But let's explore some of the things to think about and consider about sex so you can make an informed, empowered decision about what's best for you.

One of the reasons why it's so important to think these things through is because of social pressure. Schools are a hotbed of it. Everyone seems to be talking about it. It can sometimes seem like all anyone talks about is related to sex. Who's got with who. Who's done what. Where? How long? Was it good? Were they good? Who has lost their virginity?

Years of queers

Historically, there were different ages of consent. In 1967, when homosexual acts were first partially decriminalized, the age of consent between two men was originally twenty-one in the UK. This was then lowered to eighteen in 1994, and it was finally made to be equal with the heterosexual age of consent (sixteen) in 2000.

The myth of the "Big V"

In a chapter about sex, we have to discuss virginity and "losing your virginity". There are a lot of myths and rumours that go around, but I want to say this straight up here, the whole notion of losing your virginity is WEIRD. Frankly, it's outdated, sexist and as problematic as hell. It has its roots in a really old-fashioned belief that women needed to be virgins and "untouched" before marriage and that if they weren't virgins they were "impure". A load of patriarchal nonsense, eh? On top of that, it often feels like you can't win (women especially) — choose not to have sex and you're "frigid" or uptight, choose to have sex and you're a slut or easy. Sexism at its finest!

Choosing to have sex, with who and when is an important thing — but let me say here, what you choose to do (or choose not to do) with someone, any form of intimacy, has absolutely zero bearing on you or your character. While it may seem like it's a BIG DEAL and people are obsessed with talking about it, sex doesn't change you as a person, your worth or your value. And that's a really important thing to remember — it doesn't change you at all, it means nothing good or bad about you (or someone else!) whether you've done it or whether you haven't. So the idea that you are "losing your virginity" is a myth, you aren't losing anything.

Beyond the birds and the bees

Some people would have you believe sex is just when a penis goes into a vagina and that penetrative sex is the be-all and end-all. That's wrong. Sexual activity can involve a myriad of different things and is all on a spectrum (yep, that word again!). At one end, we have the PG and wholesome, and still entirely delightful, handholding (which I still love) and yep, we have kissing, then "French" kissing (what makes it French, I wonder?) and making out, spooning (when two people are cuddled up) and sporking (like spooning, but when one of those spoons gets a bit excited and suddenly grows a prong, becoming a spork). There's frotting too — fully clothed rubbing and rolling around together.

Then the clothes start to come off and things get decidedly less PG with hand jobs and fingering (whether that's vaginal or anal), oral sex (again, whether that is with a penis, a vagina or an anus) taking place. Often — but by no means always — these will lead to penetrative sex. All of these are a type of enjoyable sex you can have at some point. Or not, if that's your choice and what you think you'd prefer.

It's important to point out that there are plenty of people from different genders and sexualities who choose not to have sex. That is a perfectly valid choice.

We've also talked about asexuality, which is still a sexuality and equally deserving of respect and understanding — there's nothing weird about people who don't want it, it doesn't mean they have a low libido or there's something wrong with them, it's just not their cup of tea. If you think that might be you — don't stress, there is a whole world of asexual friendly dating out there.

Whatever appeals to you is what sex is for you (again, if you're asexual and your jam is cuddling and holding hands — go for it. You cuddle away and enjoy it!). For example, there are plenty of adult gay men who actually find that they prefer not to have penetrative anal sex and do everything else (that's why they're known as "sides", because they enjoy all the "side" bits), lots of lesbians find that penetrative sex isn't what they're into either. This just isn't what we hear about often.

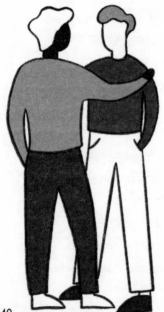

Of course, the juicy bit (lol) is the penetrative sex — that's the stuff school corridors gossip about, playgrounds share myths about, parents and teachers try to awkwardly teach us about. But nearly all of that focuses on boy-girl "don't get someone pregnant!" scare stories. Here we are also going to focus on queer sex and intimacy.

Find your flavour

When I started having sex, I didn't know how to have
the conversations around it, not just with other people
(my friends and sexual partners) but also, crucially,
I wasn't sure how to have conversations about sex
with myself. One of the greatest breakthroughs in
understanding my own sexuality (and the sex we
have, is such an important and self-affirming part of
our sexuality) was coming to think of sex as an ice
cream shop.

Imagine it – you enter your favourite ice cream
shop, let's call it Jen & Berries, and look at the many
different flavours laid out in the chiller cabinet in front
of you. There are some flavours you recognize (vanilla,
for example) and other more curious or unusual
flavours you haven't tried or maybe haven't even heard
of before. Now, you know you like ice cream (sex), but
how are you going to discover your favourite flavour
(type of sex) if you don't experiment a bit and try a
few different types along the way? Vanilla, strawberry,
chocolate brownie, cookie dough, fudge, coffee (even
pistachio!) are all fun flavours of ice cream.

You'll have your own favourites, too, and other people will have theirs but in this sexy ice cream parlour, remember a few important things:

1. The flavour of ice cream you like doesn't really matter, it's all ice cream.
2. Whatever is your favourite flavour is great for you — others don't have to like it and you don't have to like their favourite flavour either. Don't eat ice cream you don't enjoy.
3. Sometimes you'll have ice cream by yourself, sometimes you'll share it with another person. Both are good, it just depends on your mood.
4. Ice cream is not something to feel guilty about, it's perfectly harmless and pretty damn tasty.
5. Sometimes, you might not fancy having any ice cream, even if all your other friends are. You don't have to try it if you don't want to.
6. Enjoying ice cream, is nothing to feel guilty, embarrassed or ashamed of. We enjoy it because it tastes good, there's nothing wrong with that.

Advice for allies

As an ally, it's really important that you understand that the sex part (as in the actual doing it) of our sexuality is really important. Historically, it was a big battleground for our community, and even today it still comes with a whole load of shame, stigma and fear attached to it. Increasingly, it is getting sanitized out of our identity to make queer people more palatable to straight audiences. So how do you support someone when it comes to sex? Embrace this simple rule: never yuck someone else's yum.

The flavour of ice cream that they like may not be your preferred flavour, but that doesn't mean you need to yuck it. Yucking the flavour your friend is into can make them feel shame and embarrassment about what they like, which ultimately feeds into feeling shame for themselves and their choices.

On top of that, when we yuck someone else's yum (especially queer flavours of ice cream) it actually instils a homophobic hierarchy that subconsciously says "only certain flavours are tolerated", which is not unconditional support. Remember, they're not forcing you to eat their ice cream, you enjoy your favourite flavour, and let them enjoy their ice cream in peace.

Literal self-love

Whatever you want to call it – wanking, jerking, frigging – masturbation is a fact of life and something nearly everyone does. Often, it's our only experience of sex for a long time and it is a totally valid form of sexual release and expression in itself. No, it doesn't make you go blind, make the palms of your hands grow hairy, make an angel lose its wings (seriously?) or any of those other weird things grown-ups say to try and scare and shame us into not doing it. It can be an important way to get to know your own body, what kind of thing you do like, but also a way of deepening your own relationship with yourself and your body.

Masturbation releases happy hormones and makes us feel good – yes, that means it can be a form of literal self-care! Take your time, enjoy it in private and experiment with what feels good for you, take the opportunity to get to know your body for yourself. Oh yeah, and remember to clean up after yourself!

Looking after you: loving the skin you're in

One of the best things you can do for your sex life (for now and for the future) is to start to work on your relationship with your body, your acceptance of it, appreciation of it and your love for it. In the era of filters, accessible surgery, celebrity transformations and editing apps, it can be really tough to feel good and confident in your skin.

Trust me, I've been there. I've spent summers absolutely sweating like hell in sweltering heat because I felt too self-conscious to take my top off on the beach. I've looked on in envy as others have danced with gay abandon (don't worry if you had to google this phrase, it's an old saying for doing something very enthusiastically, I'm just singlehandedly trying to bring it back because I LOVE the idea of being enthusiastically gay) in tiny clothes and wished I could be like them. I've let my hang-ups about my body get in the way of relationships and moments of intimacy.

What I've learned with the years was that these were my issues with my body. Nobody else noticed the things that I felt ashamed of, and the same will be true for you. On the next page is some of the best advice that I can give you for improving your relationship with your body and how you feel about yourself.

- **Lead with appreciation:** it's too easy to pick ourselves apart for what we are not. We don't spend enough time appreciating our bodies for the wonderful things that they are and all the things they let us do. They get us around, they let us explore the world, dance and hug our loved ones. Appreciating your body will lead to a positive impact on how you feel about it.

- **Treat yourself:** our bodies work so hard for ourselves that we need to treat them well and reward them to say thanks. We can put them through a lot – dieting to change them (personally, I am not a fan of diet culture – but that's an entire other book), working out to build them, shaving them, waxing them, etc. Our bodies often need some TLC – and they really deserve it. Sometimes, treating yourself and your body to delicious and nutritious foods that make us feel good is the treat we deserve. Sometimes, that's pampering ourselves with a nice bath, face mask and moisturizer. Sometimes, it's even seducing and treating ourselves to a bit of a posh wank with some low lighting, taking our time to enjoy our body (savouring the solo ice cream), finding ways to say thank you through pleasure.

Understanding porn

Porn is pretty inescapable. It's everywhere on the Internet. In fact, the NSPCC (the National Society for the Prevention of Cruelty to Children) reckons that ninety-four per cent of people will have seen Internet porn by the time they're fourteen (though, obviously, the legal age for porn consumption is eighteen). Porn can be great, enjoyable and a useful, low-risk way of finding out what flavour of ice cream might be something you want to try — but it's also not real.

Porn is edited, stage-managed, done with professional lighting and filmed by actors (many of whom don't even identify as queer!) who are cast because of their physical appearance and prowess (overwhelmingly white, muscular, hairless and well-endowed — be that with fake breasts or well above average penis size). When you watch the Olympics, you don't compare yourself to the professional athletes, so remind yourself that porn actors (and they really are acting) are just like sexual athletes, cast for their skill and prowess that most of us just won't measure up to — no matter how much we might train.

Porn also edits out the awkward moments (smells and noises will happen — fanny and butt farts are real and common), it never shows a male performer struggling with an erection (something that affects thirty-five per cent of men under 30, and higher amounts the older we are). My lesbian mates howl with rage at the number of female performers in so-called lesbian porn — often shot and directed by heterosexual men for a heterosexual male audience – who have long fingernails. Porn also shows a very narrow range of genitalia that ignores that every penis, every vagina and every butthole is slightly different – just like snowflakes, they're special and unique (think about that next time you try and catch a snowflake on your tongue!). Magically, everyone is also always ready and prepared for anal sex, with never any conversation about "Oh wait, gimme twenty minutes – I need to douche", "Now? But I just had a pretty heavy meal" or "Um, I'm feeling pretty gassy right now". I can personally vouch that I have said ALL of these things – the first time you might feel the embarrassment but it's just our bodies, it's natural.

One of the most rewarding and pleasurable parts of sex isn't actually the physical penetration. Nor is it the act of bits and pieces going in and out or rubbing against one another. It's the intimacy that is made and shared that can be truly mind-blowing and make your heart burst. Sometimes, the closeness of lying in someone else's arms, completely content and at peace, with your breathing syncopated and limbs entangled is the really magical bit. And that never gets featured in porn! Perhaps because the action is happening on the inside, where the cameras can't see. Perhaps it's because it involves emotions – and traditional porn entirely leaves out the emotions at play and present during sex. Perhaps it's because this wonderful intimacy can even happen with our clothes on, happily holding someone's hand and losing track of time, and doesn't even need to involve physical penetrative sex.

But the most unrealistic parts of porn?

They never talk about consent.

And they never discuss safe sex.

Consent

Throughout this book, you may have noticed that I keep talking about boundaries. And never is it more important to respect your boundaries than when it comes to things like kissing, physical intimacy and sex. Sadly, I wish I was younger when I'd learned this, so I share it with you now — nobody is entitled to your body. Your body is yours to do with as you please and you do not owe it to anybody. This is where consent comes in. Consent is both an important thing to give, to withhold when we choose to and also to receive from our partners — because it goes both ways.

The guidelines to follow for consent are that it should be:

- **Enthusiastic:** if you, or your partner, are not enthusiastic about giving that yes — time to put the brakes on.

- **Clear:** "Oh, um, I guess" — hardly enthusiastic but also, it's not clear what you're agreeing to.

- **Verbal:** sometimes a nod will do. If you're on the phone and trying to indicate you would like a cup of tea, then yes please, nod away! But a nod, simply put, is not sufficient enough for bigger things. If someone doesn't feel comfortable and confident saying yes out loud, they probably don't feel comfortable or confident about doing it either.

- **Unpressured:** we've all been there, you're eating a pack of sweets and your mate asks for one, you say no. They ask again, you still say no. They ask a third time and, just to end the hassle, you say "Oh, go on then". But pressuring someone is no way to get into their sweetie bag (literal or metaphorical). If someone is pressuring you and doesn't respect your first no, that's a CLEAR sign that they're not going to take into account your wishes or needs during it. The more someone pressures you, the more that should be a reason to say no. Similarly, if someone says no to you, accept it. Don't try to guilt trip, pressure or shame them.

- **Free to be withdrawn at any time:** we are all free to change our mind and it is never too late to say so. Just because you may have started, doesn't mean you have to see it out. Every moving vehicle has brakes for a reason in case something goes wrong and we need to stop. Applying the brakes is a safety measure.

- **Shame free:** there is NOTHING bad, embarrassing or shameful about saying no. In fact, it's actually an empowered and self-respectful answer that prioritizes yourself and what you want and need.

- **Repeated:** just because someone has said yes once before, doesn't mean it's a guaranteed yes another time. Consent needs to be given each time.

- **Specific:** just because we've said yes to one thing, we haven't said yes to everything. Different acts still need to be consented to. It's not a one "Yes" covers all situation.

Remember, no means no, and is a complete sentence. You, or others, do not need to add a reason or excuse – no is your right and your answer.

Safe sex online

There is a strange quirk in the law that, at the age of sixteen, you can legally have sex, but you can't film yourself doing so (nor watch pornography either). Sex tapes and pics are, at this point, ingrained in our culture and can be part of how we flirt, build up to sex and enjoy ourselves. Some adults choose to do this when they're old enough, because when you're not pressured and you're doing it for fun it can be a great way to celebrate your body — but it should always be your choice and yours alone. But even at the ages sixteen and seventeen, while you can do the deeds, you can't document them and any pictures (even those that allegedly "disappear") count as child pornography, for which there are serious and heavy consequences. When considering taking any nude pics (and unfortunately, there will be a time when someone asks) just remember:

- If you do not want to, no is the only answer you need. Remember, no is a complete answer and a valid one that you are entitled to give with no apology attached.

- If you are under eighteen, BOTH of you could face legal problems (one for "making and disseminating", the other for having the image). While you may consent, in the eyes of the law you can't consent to this.

- These things never disappear. Just look at the number of celebrity leaks that happen. Your body is not something to be ashamed of, it is special and that means that it should be up to you to decide who gets to view it. The problem with sending a picture is that then it's out of your control and you no longer get to decide who gets to see it, in what context or what is done with it.

Saying "Yes"

There will be, at some point, a time when you might want to say yes — and that's a wonderful thing. But when is that point? That is up to you — mostly. There is a point of law we need to talk about: the legal age of consent in Britain is sixteen.

This means that any sexual activity before sixteen can have quite serious legal consequences. The age of consent means that somebody under sixteen cannot consent to having sex under any circumstances (no matter how clear, verbal or willing). Breaches of this law can carry heavy punishments, up to fourteen years in prison (if the "perpetrator" is over eighteen) or up to five years if both are under sixteen. It doesn't matter if you or they are fifteen years and 360 days old — until your sixteenth birthday, keep it PG and family-friendly.

While the law states that sixteen is the age of consent, we know that underage sex does happen. I don't advocate for it, but I want you to be prepared for what may come at you.

The first time

We know what the law states, but that doesn't mean
you have to immediately start doing it on your sixteenth
birthday — some people choose to wait until they're a little
older, some people choose to wait until they're much older.
Some even wait for marriage, while others choose to get
it over and done with. There is no hard and fast rule — and
if you've been paying attention to this book so far, you
can guess what I'm going to say: you are the only person
who'll know when it's the right time for you. I want you to
feel free, confident and empowered to choose the time,
and the how, that is right for you. Whether that is waiting
for "the one", waiting for a memorable occasion
or wanting to start getting on with it!

Marc Thompson

I would say take your time. There is so much to discover and
enjoy, there is no need to rush into everything. There is no need
to have or be pressured into sex before you're ready. I made
friends with people AFTER having sex with them and while I
don't regret that I think it's less complicated if you sometimes
leave the sex out of it.

How to be good at sex

OK – here's the real juice. How to be good at sex. It's something we all want to achieve, and it comes down to one thing ... listening. A good lover listens to who they're with, pays attention to their wants and needs, makes them feel comfortable and views the experience as about mutual pleasure, safety and shared experience. But what about for yourself? Don't put the pressure on yourself to have to be "good" – be present in it, savour the flavour and remember, even when ice cream is "bad", it's still pretty damn tasty. As long as you both leave feeling safe, happy and respected – that's a good ice cream party.

Sex admin

Sex admin? Sex? Admin? What? No, I don't mean making a spreadsheet of everything you've ever done, with whom, when and for how long, each colour coordinated in its own column. I mean acquiring and using protection, deciding on and starting birth control and STI (sexually transmitted infections) tests.

The most important thing in all of this is that you approach it in an informed way so that you can make an empowered and intelligent decision about what is right and best for you. And part of that involves the health and safety logistical stuff, which is why I've asked someone whose job it is to talk about sex to explain more.

Hi, I'm Amy from It Happens Education and we say, "it happens ... so let's talk about it." Our team of professionals help students, teachers and parents learn and talk about inclusive, positive Relationships, Sex and Health Education (RSHE). In schools, we work with students of all ages – we listen to all the amazing questions, hear all the complexities and try to untangle it all in a frank and honest way so everyone is a little bit more informed and safer out there.

It is OK to have a head full of questions about sex stuff and lots of feelings whizzing around. Unfortunately, the reproduction lessons at school don't often give young people the answers they want (and deserve) – those biology lessons (which only seem to focus on the penis-in-vagina moment) aren't really about the sort of "sex" people have most of the time. Sex is much more about the humans connected to the body parts; their desires, feelings and intimacies. If we believe that intimacy is about connection, bonding and pleasure, then sex is as much about people's heads and hearts as it is about their body parts. And sex is just so many different things to so many people.

That's why our work deals more with the feelings, thoughts and worries – the crushes, the fancies and lusts – navigating the emotional and the psychological side of communication, consent and connection. And for us, pleasure is a big part of this conversation. It might be awkward and a bit weird at first, but it shouldn't be uncomfortable or painful – this sex stuff is supposed to be enjoyable!

It's difficult to know how to talk about something so big and complex in just ten tips, but here is our guide to help you understand a bit more about bodies and boundaries.

1) Good communication: Communicating happens in so many different ways, through our words, our texts, our eyes, our touch, our breath — all the little changes in our body language. It can be verbal or non-verbal. One of the ways of working out if a partner is the right person to get intimate with is to check out your communication skills. It can be difficult sharing our innermost feelings, but communication is key for an honest and healthy relationship.

2) Understand complex consent: We have been practising consent from day one. Since we were tiny, we have been learning how to take it in turns, how to share and how to respect boundaries. You have worked a lot out about consent in friendships and hopefully understand how to respect each other. By now you probably also know that consent is not always simple and easy to understand. Humans are full of complexities! It can be so hard to work out what is really going on when feelings are overwhelming. The important question to keep asking yourself is: do you both *genuinely* have a voice and a choice? If not then you should stop.

3) Respect equality/be aware of power imbalances: It's no good if one person has all the power. Does one person do all the talking and asking and the other does all the listening and allowing? Are you both able to have ideas, to initiate and make suggestions? Are you both able to negotiate and compromise? In a clear, kind and honest way? Intimacy should be about equality. If the power dynamic feels wonky – you need to address this ASAP!

4) Look after your body: Getting to know your body is a good thing – knowing how it looks, how it feels and how to keep it clean and hygienic. Knowing what you like and what feels pleasurable is positive and really useful for you to recognize. This isn't always easy for everyone. If you aren't comfortable with your own body you probably aren't ready to get close to someone else's body, or have them close to yours.

5) Look after their body: Being a kind and caring partner means understanding their body too. This means asking, listening and responding. What might feel good one day may not work the next day, week, month or year. Bodies and behaviours change so much from moment to moment – you need to be able to respond to their body in each and every moment, looking after each other all the way.

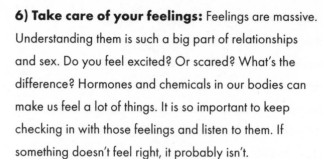

6) Take care of your feelings: Feelings are massive. Understanding them is such a big part of relationships and sex. Do you feel excited? Or scared? What's the difference? Hormones and chemicals in our bodies can make us feel a lot of things. It is so important to keep checking in with those feelings and listen to them. If something doesn't feel right, it probably isn't.

7) Take care of their feelings: Do you give them space to be honest and true about their feelings? What if they don't want to do something? What if they aren't into that idea? What if you are asking too much? How will you know? Tuning into someone else's feelings can help you to understand them and what they want and need. Sometimes people need time and space to explore their feelings on their own. Other times, they might want to share them with you.

8) Embrace the awkward moments: It's not all candles, romance, cupids and roses. Humans are complicated. This means that sometimes things might not work out exactly as planned. But that is OK. Challenging conversations need to happen. Embrace the awks. The more you learn to sit with the discomfort, and have a giggle about it, the easier it gets. And if the other person doesn't want to work though that with you then they're probably not ready to get close to you!

9) Aim for authenticity: People don't always say what they mean. Sometimes they don't mean what they say. Some folks pretend or fake it and make excuses. Others just go along with it (for lots of complicated reasons). For intimacy to be safe you need to be authentic to you. The real you. No filters, no edits, no pretending. Real feels. Real noises. Please don't pretend just cos you adore them...

10) Know where to get help: Being sexually active is a big choice. There is no obligation. It's a choice. You and your partner need to do everything you can to reduce risk by being proactive and by seeking medical support from the pros. Sexual health clinics are great, safe places to find help, and you are entitled to ask for confidentiality. We know that the legal age of consent in the UK is sixteen, but, interestingly, most sixteen-year-olds are not sexually active. What we also want you to know is that sexual health clinics will be able to help you even if you aren't quite sixteen (as long as you are over the age of thirteen). Non-judgemental medical professionals will work out how best to keep you safe. Get screened, tested and protected. Whatever it takes. Know where to get support – together!

"Together" is a big word for us. Sex isn't something you need to be a pro at or should rush into — being ready is really, really important. There are no instructions or rule books — it just doesn't work like that. It isn't something you do to someone. Or something you have done to you. In an ideal world, you and your partner will work it out together in a mature, kind, consenting, gentle and pleasurable way, and that can be connecting and very intimate!

For more information about what we do,
visit www.ithappens.education

happy
and gay

Did you know that an original meaning of the word "gay" wasn't about same-sex attraction, but was a word meaning happy?

Gay: *adjective: to be light-hearted and free.*

Yes! So, it's with a deep sense of cruel irony that I have to let you know some quite alarming figures. Unfortunately, mental health in our community is a big problem. Now, you don't need to worry – categorically, there is nothing inherent about being queer that causes any mental health issues. It's not a default setting; it's not a sign that we're wrong or defective – and certainly, being LGBTQ+ does not mean you are guaranteed to experience issues with your mental health. However, it is a real difficulty for our community – fifty-two per cent of LGBTQ+ people experience some form of mental health issue in their lifetime compared to an estimated twenty-two per cent of the general population.

As with the rest of this book, I don't tell you these things to scare or worry you. I share this with you out of a deep sense of love and compassion, trusting that, with this knowledge, you can be forewarned and better prepared as you step out into the big world. Throughout this chapter, we're going to look at ways that you help you feel light-hearted and gay. And, on those days when you don't feel so good, look at some ways you can support yourself.

Is how I feel normal?

In my day job, when I'm not writing books like this, I am a counsellor and psychotherapist. For years I've been volunteering and working in the field of mental health and so, in my professional (and personal) opinion, it is not a problem with *being queer* that causes us to be more at risk of mental health issues, it is *society's problem* with queerness that creates this risk. By that, I mean the shame, stigma, aggression and marginalization lumped upon our community for generations, has side-effects ... one of those is the impact upon our collective mental health.

Think of it like this — there is *nothing* in the genetics of someone with red hair that predisposes them to depression or anxiety ... and yet a study has shown that people with ginger hair are more likely to feel these emotions. Why? Because of the ridiculous anti-ginger school bullying that goes on and the emotional pressure they are put under, they're more likely to feel anxiety and depression as a result. Sound familiar?

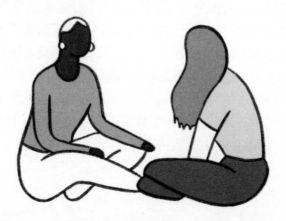

What is gay shame?

For generations, we've had cultural, religious and political judgement heaped upon us – and, unfortunately, that's left its mark. If we think back to those lovely left-handers – there's nothing wrong with being left-handed but if everybody and every institution tells you that people who are left-handed are sinful and depraved, you're going to start feeling ashamed of being left-handed.

Gay shame is that residual inner voice, the inner homophobe, who is like a horrible playground bully that's learned its prejudice from other people. But why is that so powerful? Well, shame is one of the most toxic and dangerous emotions that people can feel, it has long-lasting effects on our self-worth and how we see and think of ourselves.

Gay shame and internalized homophobia are one reason why there's gay-on-gay judgement of people who are "too" flamboyant, effeminate and camp – this is known as femme-phobia. It's not that there is anything inherently wrong with any level of campness – it's that, for some, it triggers their inner feelings of shame. In turn, we shame and judge ourselves – often internalizing and believing the corrosive thoughts of us being unworthy of love and fair treatment. Often, we police ourselves and stifle our own self-expression and happiness for fear of our own judgement, and the judgement of others.

yourself, but it also connects you to like-minded people and helps you find a place where you belong. Doing something good for someone else, like volunteering for an LGBTQ+ cause, gives a sense of pride, of worth and of value that can't be bought. Getting stuck in, joining an LGBTQ+ youth group (whether IRL or online) and finding ways to help your community can really help yourself, too. All you need to do is search online for volunteer programmes in your local area, or Young Stonewall is a fantastic place to start.

Looking after you: the joy diamond

The reality is that there will be down days – we're only human. And that's OK – sadness, moments of anxiety and depression are inevitable parts of life.

Everyone experiences them at some point, regardless of their sexuality. We can't remove them from our lives, but we can give ourselves the best chances of facing them and managing them, and we can do that by setting ourselves up in the best way possible.

A "life hack" that I like is to create a tick list for myself – it's simple, I promise! All you have to do is try to tick off a bunch of things each day from what I call "the joy diamond". To help you build up your chances of having a great day, try and tick off one of the things from each box. You can use this example that I created for myself, or try making your own.

These make serotonin, which stabilizes our mood.

These create dopamine that helps us think more clearly.

Balance

- Meditation
- Journaling
- Enjoy nature and sunshine
- Gentle exercise – give yoga a try and practise your breathing, too

Reward

- Complete a task – start small, like making your bed, then build up to bigger ones.
- Practise self-care activities
- Eat nutritious food
- Celebrate those wins

Love

- Dance to music
- Be kind to others
- Give compliments
- Hug a friend

Release

- Watch your favourite comedy and LOL
- Enjoy some dark chocolate
- Exercise – aerobic exercise, such as a quick walk or gentle run
- Smell something you like – try perfume or even freshly baked bread!

These release oxytocin, making us feel loved.

These release endorphins, helping us to feel happy and positive.

Don't worry if you struggle with this activity. Sometimes when we feel low, we need to give ourselves a little reboot. It helps to go back to our basic needs and focus on making sure those are well met, allowing us to get going again. If you're having a bad day and feeling down, check in with yourself:

Have you had enough sleep?

Have you been out into daylight and fresh air?

Have you taken care of your body, washed and put on clean clothes?

Have you eaten good, nutritious food?

Doing these simple things can make a big difference in our everyday lives. From here, we can then restart and slowly try again.

The power of self-love

The next time someone says something negative that upsets you, I want you to say something good about yourself — and I really mean it. This is based on a concept that therapists call "unconditional positive regard". This is the idea of placing no judgement, condemnation or conditions for acceptance upon others, instead we simply accept and support them as they are — and we have to practise that for ourselves, too. Unconditional positive *self*-regard, is important: we have to learn to love our *selves* regardless of whether we think we're "being good" or "being bad"; whether we're "doing well" or "doing badly" at school; or whether we're "cool" or "uncool" in the eyes of other people. We have to try and accept ourselves as we are, for who we are. It's not easy, it's a lifelong piece of work, but the sooner that you start practising it, the sooner you can get that work underway.

One of the reasons why it's so important to be authentic — to be genuinely yourself and not a developed "character" or adopted persona that you may play to appease others, or to be like someone off *Drag Race* or TikTok — is that authenticity, accepting ourselves for who we are, is the bedrock of self-worth. In therapy, we call this "congruence" — whether your inner self (who you are at your core) matches with your outer self that you project to the world. The closer aligned these two are, the happier we tend to be, while the further apart these two are the more stress our minds and emotions come under. That's why "living in the closet" and denying who we are can place such a high emotional toll on us. Similarly, copying someone else's mannerisms or their way of presenting and talking isn't going to make us feel better, it can actually make us feel worse — as if people only like us if we're not our genuine, authentic selves. And that's wrong. Your genuine, authentic self is so loveable, you just have to fall in love with that special person inside of you first.

Does all this mean we're devoid of any flaws and have no bad bits about ourselves? No. The reality is we're all human, we've all got some bits about us that aren't so great. But beating ourselves up for our shortcomings only makes us feel worse. We can end up using our energy having a go at ourselves, rather than doing what we can to grow, develop and learn. By being compassionate and kind to yourself you give yourself the best chance of becoming the best you possible.

Other people and our moods

Honestly, navigating other people can be difficult — they can be annoying and, sometimes, just plain ignorant. One of the most frustrating parts of it is that if we want others to be accepting of us, we have to be accepting of them. To be clear, I do not mean accepting someone else's bad treatment of you — that is NOT something you have to accept. But we do have to accept that we can't change or control others. We can only change and control ourselves. I like to think of it as a journey:

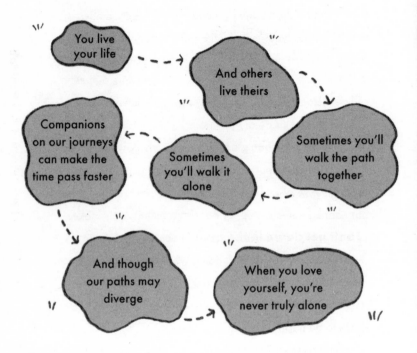

Relationships with others do not have to be built upon obligation, expectation and demands. They should be built upon mutual acceptance – acceptance of ourselves and of others. When we find those people, it's beautiful. And some people don't accept us, it can't be helped, but that is not our fight to change them. Instead, we move on, knowing that we accept ourselves and that is powerful – that is self-love.

Bullying

Sadly, bullying is an incredibly prevalent experience. A horrible one that can have long-term effects. Understandably, it can also have a big impact on how you're feeling, your mood and your confidence. Here are some tips that can help you if you're being bullied.

Talk. Talking to somebody about how you're feeling, whether that is a favourite teacher, a supportive parent, a trusted friend or a support line, is a great way to release some of the pressure, find support and work through your emotions.

Don't get down in the mud. It's really, *really* unfair that the burden to "do the right thing" falls onto the person who has been wronged and picked on. But, as the old saying goes, two wrongs don't make a right. You have to be happy with your own behaviour, and stooping as low as someone else will only make you feel worse. Hold your head high and know that retaliation will only make you as bad as them. It feels unfair, but it's true.

Disengage. When something is hot, we don't touch it – don't burn yourself by engaging when there's a fire raging. Be empowered in your right to walk away from heated conversations and situations – both in real life and on social media. You don't have to read everything.

Turning your phone off and putting it away is a great way to set boundaries and give yourself some distance.

Understand. Understand that happy, confident and secure people don't bully others. Happy people don't need to tear others down. If someone is bullying you, this is often a reflection of how they feel about themselves and what scares them. It doesn't make it right; it doesn't make it fair — but know that your confidence and authenticity is what scares them because they're jealous of you. You've done nothing wrong.

Find outlets for your emotions. Don't bottle up all the sad feelings, write them down, journal, cry them out, talk them through, sing along LOUDLY to a punk song. Whatever you do, just don't leave feelings to build up inside of you — remember, when dams let out water in a controlled way, it creates power and turns the lights on. What can you do to help channel the power inside of you to help fuel you on?

Cherish yourself. When someone else is putting you down, it is EVEN MORE important to big yourself up, to treat yourself, to celebrate yourself and to take care of yourself. *Every* time they say something bad about you, immediately either write down or say something good about you and repeat it at least three times. I'm serious, this has been proven to work!

Advice for allies

Everybody has mental health. And we all have challenges – when we're facing these challenges, that's the most important time for our allies to stand with us and help share some of the burden. So, there are a few principles I want us all to adopt into our lives:

Never be a bystander. Whether you are seeing someone being bullied, or think that someone may be going through a hard time emotionally, never passively observe it. Not doing or saying anything leaves them in their moment of need alone. That's the most important time to step up and take a stand.

Ask twice. We can brush things off when someone reaches out to us, so asking twice is a great tip. "How are you?", *"I'm fine"*, "How are you *really*? Because I noticed X/Y/Z and I wondered how you were feeling..." Give them an opportunity to reach out, show them it's a safe space.

Don't be scared. We can put a lot of pressure on ourselves to make sure we say the right thing, but the reality is we have to say very little – making space for them to talk and feel supported is the most powerful thing.

Loving the skin you're in

Learning to love and value yourself can take time, but it's important to celebrate you and everything that makes you unique.

Mohsin Zaidi, Author, Barrister and Speaker (he/him)

I was bullied every day at school. I was told to be thick skinned and ignore the bullies. But every tiny moment of name-calling or violence stripped away a layer of that skin. What I found underneath was a strong, powerful person and, eventually, you will too.

I am Pakistani and I am gay. I am proud of both these parts of my identity. Don't let anyone tell you that any two or more parts of your identity cannot co-exist. The fact that you exist means that they can.

Kayza Rose

First, getting to know yourself is a lifelong process, you'll change as time goes on, this is OK. Take what you find along the way as examples of being. Some will feel like home and some won't, this is OK. You also have the right to change your mind at any time, allowing yourself to grow is healing and challenging at the same time. Don't let anyone rush you or project their own motives onto you. Your feelings and needs are valid. Try different spaces, different groups, don't feel obliged to stay in a space that makes you feel shame or is unsafe occupying your visible or invisible intersections.

Jason Kwan

I was bullied quite a lot at school both in Hong Kong and in the UK. How I coped was by realizing that their opinions of me were not a true reflection of me, but a reflection of their insecurities. I surrounded myself with the things I love, including music, pop culture, reading and my friends. Make sure you can carve out a space where you feel safe in, and that belongs to you.

Liam Hackett, Author and Founder and CEO of the anti-bullying charity Ditch the Label (he/him)

Trust me, as somebody who experienced bullying throughout most of my time at school, I know that it can be one of the hardest and loneliest experiences. It's hard to imagine that almost half of all your classmates experience it at some point, so you really aren't alone. If you're experiencing bullying, for whatever reason, the most important lesson I learned is that it's important to not blame yourself. You are perfect as you are and you shouldn't ever shrink, change or hide parts of yourself in order to make other people feel better. Hold your head up high, stay strong and remember that this situation is temporary. You are never alone and there is so much support available to you.

Yasmin Benoit

You march to the beat of your own drum and people don't know how to handle that. That doesn't mean that you need to change or dim your light, it means that other people need some time to catch up. And it'll happen in time. Stay true to yourself, you'll find your rhythm and you'll be surprised by how many end up dancing along in the future.

Your power will protect you

However we identify, wherever we're from, whatever we look like, there will, unfortunately, be people who try to come for us and tear us down. In recent years, thanks in part to social media, it has begun to feel like any public discourse is just people YELLING back and forth at one another, trying to shout the other down, name calling, shame and score points.

Our phones have only thrown fuel on this fire, bringing hate from the streets and school into our homes and bedrooms, carried in our pockets. But remember, you don't have to read everything or engage — switching off, disengaging from threads and fights is an act of strength, not cowardice.

One of the greatest powers you have to protect yourself is to love yourself. I keep banging on about it because it is so important, it is so special and it is so powerful. In the face of any adversity that life throws at you, cherishing, celebrating and loving yourself is the best defence.

Your worth is not defined by the clothes you wear, how you look, how many followers or likes you have. Really, what matters is your opinion of yourself. We can too easily be our own worst critic when, really, we should be our own best friend and cheerleader.

Your story

One of the first things that humankind ever did was tell stories – it's something we've done for thousands of years because stories have power. That includes the stories we tell ourselves. These stories are powerful and can have a big impact upon our hearts, minds and the way we see the world.

It's important to think about the story we tell ourselves and to be mindful of how we label our emotions and experiences. Accidentally writing our narrative to have a negative slant is very easy to do if we don't watch our words. Good mental health is not an absence of all negative emotions (they're a part of life), nobody is permanently one hundred per cent happy; we all have moments of sadness, anxiety and even times when we feel depressed – but they pass. If we always tell ourselves that we "have anxiety", then that can become a limit that we put on ourselves. This can actually mean we're far more likely to experience anxiety because we end up becoming anxious about getting anxious! We need to be careful about the story we tell ourselves and remind ourselves of the positive parts of ourselves too.

This is where practising affirmations can come in. An affirmation is a little bit like an empowering quote or mantra that you repeat to yourself. It helps set your intention and helps you set yourself with a positive narrative. The three most powerful things I want you to say to yourself are this:

I forgive you.

I accept you.

I love you.

Even if you have to start by saying them in your mind, do. Take a moment for yourself, breathe, and really focus your intention on meaning those words. Try to really feel them.

Forgiveness: forgiving yourself is important. We can carry around guilt for all sorts of things, and it will just weigh you down. But let me be clear, nothing about your sexuality or identity is in need of forgiveness. Your identity may upset somebody — but forgive yourself of any guilt that you may feel. That's not yours to carry, let it go.

Acceptance: accept yourself, for who you are, as you are — flaws and all. Your gender, expression or who you're attracted to is not a flaw. All you need to do is accept yourself as you are: as your authentic, true self.

Love: loving yourself gives you power. We can get awkward about this idea — "Oh, they love themselves!" is thrown around as a way of taking someone down. But we SHOULD love ourselves. Loving yourself is the work of a lifetime, and it's never too early to start.

Forgive your imperfections, accept yourself as you are and love yourself for you. That is how we can live happily and gayly.

Love yourself

No matter who you are, it's important to love yourself.

What do you love about yourself? Don't worry if it takes time for you to answer this question, you're worth the wait.

Elliot Douglas

Who I am is OK and has always been OK. There is no rush to know everything about yourself and parts of what make up your identity can change, grow and evolve many times over our lives.

Calling your guardian angel

This is one of my favourite exercises, I've been doing it since I was a teenager as a meditation exercise, and now since practising in a clinic I've found that it's a great way to help people protect themselves against all those nasty voices, feelings of doubt, shame or inadequacy that can sometimes creep in.

If you're not religious, that's cool. Neither am I. Don't let the phrase "guardian angel" put you off, you can call this guide whatever you like — defending spirit, mental cheerleader, it's up to you. Ready to begin?

I want you to visualize someone (or something) who is there to comfort you, support you, guard you and love you unconditionally. Maybe it's a real person that you know, your favourite pet or a celebrity that you're a big fan of, but my favourite is to create them new.

Take a moment to think about this guide, what do they look like? Are they tall and strong to guard you, or shorter

and cuddly with warm arms to embrace you? What do they wear? Is it shining armour, a dazzling and fabulous sequined dress, a billowing superhero cloak or a casual fluffy jumper? Or are they covered in fur?! Are they carrying anything? A regal sceptre, a book of knowledge, a lance of power or a Mary Poppins bag full of whatever you need? How do they sound when they talk? Strong and defiant, maybe like Elektra from *Pose*, or a warming voice? Do they have an accent? (My faves are the Geordie and Welsh accents — you can't get more friendly than those!)

Take a moment to visualize your guardian angel and really get to know them — put down this book and close your eyes if it helps. The details of who they are and what they're like are up to you — but remember that they're on your side, helping you on your journey.

Then it's time to put them to work. Anytime a voice of doubt or shame creeps in, turn to your guardian, what would they say? They're there to comfort you; cheer you on with an inspiring pep talk; support and to listen to your troubles; defend you, throwing up a powerful shield; and remind you to ignore what the haters say — you are loveable; you are worthy.

We spend too long listening to the negative voices in our heads, and the voices of others — so it's time to give the mic to the guardian you've created instead. Listen to them, turn to them, ask them for advice, hear their words of support. Believe in them. Believe in you.

pride

What do you think of when you think of pride? What does it mean to you? Perhaps not much yet, perhaps it feels very far off – even a little bit scary. Maybe it feels exciting. Perhaps you think of one specific day when joyful and exuberant queer people march in the streets. Perhaps you think of an inner feeling that's growing inside of you – PRIDE in being your honest and authentic self. Maybe, when you think of pride, you think of none of those things and it doesn't mean anything to you yet.

Emotionally – pride is a powerful feeling (the opposite of shame), where we can stand as our honest selves, feeling happy and content.

Logistically – Pride is an event held in lots of different places (although, confusingly, all on different days) to celebrate our LGBTQ+ family, culture, journey, history and presence.

Historically – Pride is the rejection of "gay shame" (which we talked about before) and a turning point in the queer political movement, and a time when we take to the streets to stand up for our collective rights.

Surrounded by others who accept me

A time to remember those who fought for us

Pride is ...

Love of one's self. Kindness. Unity.

Self-acceptance

A celebration of belonging

Feeling happy in my own skin

Not being afraid, or embarrassed, to say I'm queer

Thriving instead of surviving

Being comfortable in your own truth

Celebrating what we've all overcome

Saying no to shame

A call to love ourselves and one another

Remembering those that came before us

Refusing to be ashamed of who you are

Overcoming struggles and accepting who you are

So, what and when actually *is* Pride?

Is it a parade? Is it a party? Pride is both of those things. But, importantly, we must never forget that Pride is a protest and Pride is political. Internationally, June is recognized as Pride Month and many rallies, activities, community gatherings, protests – and yes – parties and parades happen in this month. On social media, there's always a flurry of rainbow logos and special Pride edition merch which announces Pride Month each year.

But that doesn't mean we shouldn't *feel* pride the rest of the year – it's just a specific time to recognize collectively the journey and history of our community, to come together and to remind us to always seek to push forward for equality for all. Because that's the thing – equality isn't some "one and done" thing, it is something that has to be worked at and continuously guarded.

The best way to think of it is that progress is a process. And, in actual fact, loads of Pride marches happen at totally different times! London typically holds its Pride march at the end of June or early July, while Manchester has its one in August while many other towns and cities all over the UK hold theirs on different dates. If you wanted to, you could have a very gay old time for a good few months travelling around in between the different ones! Perhaps googling to see if your local town has a Pride celebration could be a great way for you to see what community is around you.

Years of queers

You learn about Henry VIII and his six wives in school
– but it was he, as part of the English Reformation
(when England broke away from the Catholic Church),
who first criminalized homosexuality. In 1533, what
was known as "The Buggery Act" came into force and
punished male (not female) same-sex activity with
death. It wasn't until 1861 that the death penalty was
removed (and replaced with ten years of hard labour).
One of the most famous victims of the change in law
was playwright Oscar Wilde, who served time in
prison after being publicly taken to trial for same-sex
relationships.

The history of Pride

The Stonewall Riots, 28 June 1969, are popularized in
queer folklore as "the match that started the fire" of the
modern LGBTQ+ liberation movement. The story goes that
at a small queer dive bar, The Stonewall Inn in downtown
New York City, patrons were regularly harassed by police
looking to fine people and enforce America's queerphobic
laws (such as you must always wear at least three items
of your assigned gender's clothing). One night, the police
pushed too hard, and the punters at The Stonewall Inn
fought back. Legend has it that Marsha P. Johnson and

Sylvia Rivera, two trans women of colour, were the first to stand up – throwing a drink (or a shoe) at the police and triggering five days of riots by Manhattan's put-upon LGBTQ+ community.

There's just a bit of a problem with our retelling of this, aside from a lot of it not actually being true – Sylvia Rivera herself denied her involvement for a long time and Marsha P. Johnson by her own admission wasn't there the night the riots started – it over-simplifies a very long, very complicated struggle that was undertaken by many people, in many places and over a very long time.

If we look at Marsha and Sylvia, people talk about their involvement in the riots, but the rest of their lifelong activism is very rarely discussed. Marsha was a tireless activist and community organizer who continuously fought for our rights, founding the Gay Liberation Front (GLF) and, together with Sylvia Rivera, they co-founded the Street Transvestite Action Revolutionaries. Their work, the change they created and their legacy was more than one night; it was something they did (literally) for decades. The mythology around Stonewall is powerful, and it was undeniably an important moment, but the concern is this – by overplaying the myth of it, we can mistake what activism is and how progress is made. Progress and change take time, it takes a lot of brave people doing countless hours of work, organization within our community and taking care of one another. It takes all of us, and the work is still not done.

Stonewall was powerful and important, but let's not forget about all the other steps that were taken along the way.

Pride in people power

1954 – The Homosexual Law Reform Society (HLRS) was formed by a coalition of academics to push for the decriminalization of homosexuality. Importantly, many of these people were allies and supported our cause long before it was "safe" to do so.

1957 – The Wolfenden Report. A government enquiry into homosexuality argued in favour of the decriminalization of homosexuality. Three brave men gave public evidence as to how the law had impacted their lives. Their names were Peter Wildeblood, Carl Winter and Patrick Trevor-Roper. Despite the risk to their personal safety and careers, they refused their right to anonymity (as offered by the government) stating that they had "nothing to be ashamed of" – that sounds a lot like the beginnings of Pride to me. Some years later, the son of the committee's chair (John Wolfenden) would come out as homosexual, raising the question, perhaps the love one father had for his own son was behind the legal change in our rights.

1966 – The Beaumont Society was founded. It was the UK's first transgender support group and it is still thriving today.

1969 – The Campaign for Homosexual Equality was founded, a grassroots organization pushing for societal change and equality for lesbians, gay men and bisexuals throughout the UK. This then morphed into the GLF which became the UK's first radical street activism group who were loud and unapologetic in their demands. It focused on emancipating queer people from repression and called on all queers to come out and stand proud.

1972 – 1 July 1972, the first UK Gay Pride March took place (organized by the GLF) and 1,000 people marched from Trafalgar Square to Hyde Park. It was a true protest, with the brave members of that march receiving heckles and jeers from the crowd – and still they marched on.

1982 – The Gay Black Group (GBG) was founded and pushed for greater racial equality and the end of racism within the gay and lesbian community. In 1985, they opened the Black Lesbian and Gay Centre, providing advice, counselling, community groups, a support line and a community library. Today, their legacy is upheld with the brilliant UK Black Pride.

1982 – The Terrence Higgins Trust is founded as the UK's first AIDS charity. Named after Terry Higgins, one of the first people in Britain to die from AIDS, his partner and friends set up the campaigning and support organization. It still runs today and has saved and changed countless lives through its advocacy, support and fundraising for HIV and AIDS.

In **1988**, Section 28 was a piece of legislation enacted by the then Conservative government (under Margaret Thatcher) to ban "the promotion of homosexuality". This meant that for many years – even as late as 2010 in some parts of the country despite its partial repeal in 2003 – anybody paid out of the public purse was banned from discussing LGBTQ+ issues and support. For example, this meant libraries couldn't carry any helpful information (this book would've been banned) and teachers weren't able to teach equal rights, LGBTQ+ equality or even have anti-homophobic or transphobic bullying policies.

1989 – In response to Section 28, UK queer politics steps up a gear. As legendary human rights activist Peter Tatchell says, "Section 28 was the bomb under gay rights". Attendance at Pride jumped from 15,000 people, pre-Section 28, to 30,000 the year the law came in, 100,000 the next and even as high 300,000 LGBTQ+ people and allies taking to the streets.

Europe's largest LGBTQ+ campaign group and charity, Stonewall UK, was set up by a group of activists, including Sir Ian McKellen (aka Gandalf!), in direct opposition and response to Section 28. Brilliant grassroots activism and protest work was undertaken by thousands of members of the community — including the awesomely named Lesbian Avengers who parasailed into the Houses of Parliament down a washing line to disrupt MPs from voting and even interrupted a live *BBC News* broadcast screaming, "STOP SECTION 28!"

1995 — Mermaids is founded to support young trans children and their families, lobbying for their rights and providing education and support for families. It's still the only UK charity for trans youth today.

So you can see, change has been made over a long period of time, by countless people, many of whom go unnamed and unrecognized. The fight still goes on to this day, newer organizations like Opening Doors, Lesbians and Gays Support the Migrants, ExistLoudly, Not A Phase and UK Black Pride have been born and carry on the cause. There are many more groups, organizations and people that aren't referenced here (just simply because that would be an entire book in itself!) but every one is something to be proud of. A good question to ask yourself is: how will I get involved?

Kayza Rose

Take up space, scream the loudest. Don't take up space, be quiet. Be an activist, don't be an activist. Take up space on your own terms, you do not have to be the voice or representation for people that look like you. This may not be your calling; this is totally OK. Your Blackness and queerness are you, not a performance of you. You are valid just as you are, even if that's being quiet and getting on with your life with nobody else knowing what you do. Don't feel responsible for educating your white/non-Black friends or colleagues, if they want a consultant, there are fees for that. Don't become that "one Black friend", you make them pay a consultancy rate, sis.

Human rights campaigner Peter Tatchell has spent his life working to support and protect the rights of marginalized individuals and communities in the UK and around the world. A champion of LGBTQ+ rights, I'm proud to be able to share his story here with you to inspire you to stand up and speak out for what you believe in.

Pay attention to how normal and human Peter's story is, having started small and worked his way up. Remember, activism can start anywhere at anytime. Activism is active in the real world, not just online, and you can share your message with other people through different platforms, from social media to protest marches. No matter how small, you can make a big difference to the lives of others by sharing your voice.

How I began my LGBTQ+ human rights campaigning

Written by **Peter Tatchell**

Wow! I have now been campaigning for human rights for over 50 years. For much of this time, I have been the lone ranger of queer politics. It is only since 2011 that I've had the backup of an organization, the Peter Tatchell Foundation. Prior to that, it was an unpaid solo crusade. My campaign resources were limited. Life was tough. I lived in poverty. But I have no regrets.

Looking back over my last five decades of activism, what I've done seems so unreal, so implausible. After all, nothing in my family background inclined or prepared me for a lifetime of LGBTQ+ and human rights campaigning.

So how did it all begin? I was born in Melbourne, Australia, in 1952; growing up in a period of illiberal government and anti-communist witch-hunts. My parents were ultra-conservative evangelical Christians, similar to those depicted by Jeanette Winterson in her book, *Oranges Are Not the Only Fruit*. Loving, but strict and narrow-minded.

My life was cosseted and suffocating. Everything revolved around the family and church. Beyond their own fairly right-wing views, my parents had no interest in politics. They were not concerned about human rights or even local community issues. They were unworldly and insular. But, on the positive side, rooted in their Christian beliefs, they taught me to stand up for what is right and to not just follow the crowd. This is a maxim that I still believe in. It has informed my human rights work, as I have often taken up just causes, like LGBTQ+ rights, that were initially marginal and had little public support.

My father, Gordon, worked in an engineering factory,

as a lathe operator. Mardi, my mother, alternated between being a housewife and working in a biscuit factory. She had bouts of chronic, life-threatening asthma. There was no NHS in Australia in those days, so much of our family income went on medical bills. We were dirt poor. Birthday and Christmas presents were meagre. Meals were basic. My clothes were sometimes secondhand and mended. This hardship probably honed my passion for justice.

From the age of eight, whenever my mother was ill, I had to run the household and bring up my younger brother and sisters – cooking and washing when I got home from school. It restricted my playtime with friends but made me independent and resourceful.

Being born a few years after the end of the Second World War, many comics, books and films had war themes. By the age of eleven, I used to ask adults: "Why did people allow Hitler to get power? Why didn't they stop him?" No one gave me a satisfactory answer. I vowed that if I ever saw tyranny and injustice, I would not remain silent and do nothing.

My first "political" awakening was in 1963 when I was eleven years old. I saw reports about the racist bombing of a Black church in Birmingham, Alabama, USA, which killed four young girls who were about my own age. I was stunned and horrified. It made me a lifelong anti-racist and inspired me to follow – and admire – Dr Martin Luther King Jr and the Black civil rights movement.

My campaigning for human rights began in 1967, aged 15, when I protested against the hanging of an alleged killer, Ronald Ryan, despite doubtful, conflicting evidence. His execution destroyed my trust and confidence in the police, courts and government and resulted in a lifetime of scepticism towards authority. It opened my eyes to other injustices: the mistreatment of the indigenous Aboriginal people and the brutal war being waged against the people of Vietnam by the US and Australian governments.

At my local high school, I was a rebel. I demanded and won the right of pupils to have a say in running the school. On 4 July 1968, I burned the US flag in the playground in protest at the Vietnam War. I also co-organized a sponsored walk by school pupils to raise money for scholarships for indigenous Aboriginal pupils who were often pressured to leave school early to financially support their families. The aim was to get them qualifications, so they could get better jobs to uplift their often impoverished communities.

I was not aware of my gayness at that time. I had good legs — the best in the school, according to some boys. They used to wolf-whistle me. I was gently teased with jibes of "poofter Pete". It didn't upset me, because I was confident that I was straight. Besides, I was popular and well-liked. My fellow pupils voted me School Captain in 1968.

That year, aged sixteen, I had to leave school to get a job to help supplement our family income. My passion was art and design. I wanted to do architecture or design but I had no qualifications. My parents could not afford to send me to university or art college. So I settled for doing design and display in a big department store. That's where I first met gay people and soon after realized that I was gay. I fell in love, aged seventeen, and began a passionate relationship. We got a flat together, which enabled me to escape my oppressive family life.

I read a report about gay liberation protests in New York in late 1969 and immediately decided that I wanted to be part of the fight for LGBTQ+ freedom. Reflecting on the Black civil rights movement, I concluded that LGBTQ+ people were an oppressed minority, just like Black people, and equally deserving of human rights – and that Martin Luther King's tactics of non-violent direct action and civil disobedience could be applied to the struggle for LGBTQ+ rights. I also calculated, again based on the experience of the Black civil rights movement, that it would take about 50 years to win LGBTQ+ legal equality in Western countries like Australia, the US and Britain. It proved to be a near-accurate guess.

There were no LGBTQ+ organizations in Melbourne back then. I had no template for how to do activism, so the US Black civil rights movement became my template. I adapted its ethics, ideals and methods to the quest for LGBTQ+ freedom.

This experience bought home to me the importance and

value of listening to, and learning from, other struggles – and supporting each other. It taught me the value of allies because in those lonely early days I needed LGBTQ+ and straight allies for moral support to sustain my campaigning.

Australia had conscription for Vietnam in that era. I was not willing to fight an unjust war. The penalty for refusal was two years in jail. So I skipped the country and came to London in 1971. Within five days, I was at my first meeting of the newly formed Gay Liberation Front. A few weeks later, I was helping to organize the GLF's feisty protests.

Modelled on the methods of the Black civil rights movement, in 1971 I helped organize sit-ins at pubs that refused to serve "queers". We got dragged out by the police but forced the pub owners to back down. We scored the same success when we protested against a Piccadilly Circus cafe that tried to turf out trans customers.

From the outset, I saw the LGBTQ+ struggle as a global one, not just limited to the UK. In 1971, I co-organized a picket of the Cuban embassy to protest against LGBTQ+ people being sent to forced labour camps by the Castro regime. Two years later, I staged the first LGBTQ+ demonstration in a communist country, the former East Germany, which got me arrested by the secret police, the Stasi. I was lucky to escape without being jailed.

That, then, was how my half a century of LGBTQ+ and other human rights activism began. The rest, is as they say, history.

What I have done is all the more remarkable given that my family background and education did nothing to incline or prepare me for a campaigning life. If I can, anyone can. I hope that my activism will inspire and motivate you to do great things in whatever field of endeavour you are working in. And remember, listen and learn from other struggles and be an ally in their battle for justice. Together, we are stronger.

Your first Pride

But what about Pride the day? The march! The party! The protest! What's it like? For me, it was beyond exciting — to go from the suffocation of my school, where I had to suppress so much of myself (even though I was out!), to suddenly seeing SO MANY people living with such joy, happiness, confidence and, yes, pride in who they were, gave me real hope. It gave me a new power inside — if so many other people had come from feeling how I felt to quite literally dancing in the streets, so could I. And so can you.

Ryan Lanji

We stand together, we laugh together, we cry together, we defy together and reimagine together. That's queer joy. That's Pride.

Top Pride survival tips

- Wear comfy shoes (you are gonna be on your feet for a LONG time!)
- Consider joining a youth organization to go with who can be your guide
- Smile — it is a time to be friendly, say hello!
- Take a small zip bag (I love a bumbag for Pride — make your own joke!) to put all your essentials in so you don't lose anything while marching and dancing
- Remember that Pride is not just a party — engage with the politics and the cause
- Honour our history, which includes saluting and supporting older LGBTQ+ members of the community

Advice for allies

Thinking of attending Pride as an ally? Of course you're welcome! Come on in! But think about attending Pride a bit like this – if you were having a birthday party and somebody showed up and started acting all loud and crazy, making your day all about them, distracting from celebrating your awesome birthday and your achievements, you'd suddenly feel like they were a lot less welcome at the party, right? Pride is like our birthday party. Don't make it about you, it's your chance to celebrate us and enjoy joining in with that.

Looking after you: dealing with overwhelming environments and nerves

It can be quite an overwhelming experience going to your first Pride – the emotion and anticipation, the sheer number of people, the bright colours and the loud music can make it all feel a bit much. What do we do to support ourselves when we feel overwhelmed? Check in with our bodies and make sure that we're present and in control of ourselves (this works for any overwhelming situations, events or times when you're nervous – even for exams!)

Regulate your breathing: breathe in slowly for four seconds, hold your breath for four seconds, then slowly exhale again for four seconds. Repeat this three more times. This is called square breathing – some people find that it helps them to visualize a square as they're doing it, where each side represents a different four-second chunk of time.

Check in with your body: how is your body feeling? Focus on your toes – the sensation of them in your socks or shoes, give them a wriggle and focus on that sensation. Then rock back and forth, engaging your feet, ankles and calves – how does that feel? Focus on each part of your body. Coming up slowly, bend your knees, then twist your waist – slowly working your way up your body and relaxing any tension that you become aware of. As you come above your waist to your torso, your back, shoulders, hands and jaw, move them slowly – these are places where you might really be holding tension and feeling tight. Focus your mind on melting away that toughness, letting your muscles go. Tell your body to release and relax. As you go on, think about whether your jaw is clenched, your brow furrowed, shoulders tense and tight – if they are, relax your body, and your mind will start to follow.

Work out your needs: now that we feel more grounded, we can ask what it was that caused us to feel overwhelmed. If it's an emotional challenge go back to the worry tree in chapter five and work out whether that is a *good* worry or a *bad* worry. If it's a worry linked to a physical state, what do you need at that moment? To move somewhere quieter that's less crowded? How about your physical needs: is your sugar level low? When did you last eat? Look out for your emotional and physical needs to get the best out of your day.

Pride is not just one day

Pride marches are powerful, amazing things. But Pride is not just one day, it lives on within all of us, as a feeling, as a way of life and in the actions we take. I talked before about how volunteering and getting involved in organizations is a great way to meet people (and that it's good for you!), but getting involved in our community, in any way that you can, is also a wonderful way to feel pride for 365 days a year.

Corporate Pride

One controversy of Pride, and often a valid criticism, is how commercial it has become. Given that it started as a political protest, demonstrations, sometimes violent clashes with police, many people find it jarring that now each summer everywhere you look there are huge corporations suddenly turning their logo rainbow themed or releasing their limited edition Pride range of cheaply printed T-shirts. OK, some of them are cute and I kind of want them, but we have to think about who's benefiting. Is our community benefiting from this or is this just a bit of marketing? Are these corporations taking our story, our history, our pride and community and using it and making it all about them? Exactly like we tell allies not to! The same rules on allyship apply to companies as they do to people.

So why can't we just do away with it all? The reality is we live in a capitalist society that is driven by money. As much as I wish we lived in a green-focused socialist world, we don't. As such, that means we have to operate within it the best we can. The LGBTQ+ community is underfunded and we need money. We need it for all sorts of causes, from education and housing support to sexual and mental health, addiction and medical care for our community. For example, trans people need properly funded healthcare but don't get it.

So, here's a question for you, and I want you to have a guess:

If we are one in ten of the population, for every £100 donated to charitable causes would you expect £10 (i.e. ten per cent) of that to go to LGBTQ+ causes?

How about £1 in every £100? One per cent of all charitable donations?

Nope. We receive only 4p out of every £100 donated to charity in Britain (according to figures released by the Trades Union Congress). That's 0.0004 per cent.

You and I, and other queer people, sadly, can't make up that shortfall – the difference is too big. And queer charities are still needed today and so – in the imperfect world that we live in – that means we have to accept corporate money. If a company wants to try and get on the Pride bandwagon, sure I'll accept it, but they better be paying a hefty price tag for it! And if they're not? Boot them out. You don't show up to a mate's house party without taking something, and they're not even our mate! They want in? They gotta pay their way.

And, no matter what they say, pride doesn't depend on buying a T-shirt, pride is within you, always.

The pride inside

You don't always have to show pride to have pride. Your arms would get tired from always waving a flag and your voice would get sore from all the chanting. But the reality is, sometimes, it's not possible to show pride. If you're unsafe, if you're nervous or alone, it is OK – that doesn't make you a bad queer. It doesn't mean you're "failing the cause" or anything like that. As long as you hold on to the knowledge that you are whole, you are worthy and you refuse to feel ashamed inside, then you live the values of Pride. Let it burn within you and help get you through, as is it did for others.

Mohsin Zaidi
It's OK to be scared. Everybody is. But one day soon overcoming that fear will become a source of strength.

Corinee Humphreys, Sprinter and Stonewall Sports **Champion, (she/her)**
Having pride means believing in your sauce and living unapologetically as the truest version of yourself. Haters are going to hate! Always believe in your sauce because every part of your identity is what makes you special in this world. On your journey of exploring your gender and sexuality, always remember to continue to explore your talents and interests. Every part of your identity makes you special.

Char Bailey, Facilitator, Speaker and Consultant (she/her)

Don't forget to come in, while you come out. Getting to know myself, love myself and trust myself has made existing in my Black and brown, neurodivergent, queer space so much easier.

Jason Kwan

Being queer, being non-binary, being part of the LGBTQ+ community means having a deeper existence. So often I question who I am, why I am the way I am and consider the different parts of my identity. This process has helped me understand myself more, understand how other people navigate the world and has helped me love myself and others more too. My queerness reverberates love, compassion and passion, and I am so proud to be part of an ever-growing community of acceptance.

Marc Thompson

Queer joy to me is freedom. It's when I/we can be totally unapologetic about who we are, the spaces we occupy, who we love and how we love and can be our truly authentic selves. It's also being on the dance floor with Black queer people in Black spaces we have created not because of the "deficit" narrative that mainstream spaces don't cater for us, but just because we can and want to.

allyship

At some point in your life, I'm sure you've been alone and outnumbered in an argument. Whether that argument was big or small, defending your point of view and what you know to be right against other people when you're outnumbered feels horrible. And it's exhausting. In that fight, I bet you would've loved to have someone take your side, to back you up, to stand with you so that you weren't alone.

You've also probably had it at some point where you've been put in a different class to your friends or had to work on a group project with people you didn't know (or like). Think about how uncomfortable, even scary, that can feel. Now imagine how much heavier those emotions must feel when it's something as important as how you identify, who you are. Rather than missing out on the gossip from class or doing a project with your friends, what is at stake is your happiness, your dignity, even your safety. It's huge.

Think of a time that you've been carrying something heavy, perhaps it's your suitcase on your way on holiday. You love all the clothes you've packed, you're excited about where you're going, but carrying it is heavy. Then somebody kindly offers to help you carry it, sharing the weight to make your journey a bit easier. That's an ally. A good ally will understand that the weight of carrying something alone can be exhausting, they won't try to steal your luggage and make your cute holiday clothes fit them

— they're just there to help.

Frankly, all causes need allies. White people need to be better, more active and less problematic allies to people of colour in the global struggle against racism; men need to call out their "laddy" mates and challenge their sexist behaviour in all-male spaces and on the streets; young people (who are going to be hardest hit by the climate crisis) need older people to put pressure on those in power. We all need allies.

Why do we need allies?

To the uneducated eye (we'll give them the benefit of the doubt), somebody might look on paper and say, "You've got anti-discrimination legislation, you've got gay marriage, you've even got a WHOLE MONTH for Pride — isn't everything fine?" But if you've been paying attention to this book, you'll have an idea — no, everything is not fine.

It's true that in a lot of the Western world we have made great progress on equal rights, but these things aren't the endpoint of our journey to equal rights, and the reality of our lives is somewhat different. Buckle up for some hard-hitting facts on the next page.

Queerphobic bullying is still the number one form of bullying in schools today. Nearly half, fourty-five per cent, of LGBTQ+ pupils experience homophobic bullying at school, which rises to sixty-four per cent of trans pupils.

A quarter of people under the age of 25 living rough on the streets are LGBTQ+. They have either been kicked out of home over their sexuality or gender identity, or have been forced to run away from an unsafe home environment.

Almost seventy per cent of queer people in Britain avoid displaying same-sex affection out of fear for their safety.

Homosexuality is still illegal in 72 countries around the world, 35 of them within the Commonwealth, and 14 countries punish it with death. By contrast, just 27 countries around the world permit same-sex marriage.

These sobering statistics aren't just cold figures, they're about real people's everyday lives. That's why challenging homophobia, transphobia, biphobia and proactively supporting all queer people around you is crucial. There is safety in numbers and we need people to stand with us. Feel free to quote these statistics at anybody who says "It's all fine now," or that the world has gone PC mad.

What is an ally?

An ally, in the traditional sense, refers to a country that pledges to help and support another, especially during a time of war or hardship, and to work together for mutual benefit. But how does this apply to people?

What does a "straight ally" do?

Well, they are *active* in their support of the LGBTQ+ community. It takes action – speaking up, changing your habits, challenging friends, showing up in times of need – not just wearing a rainbow and watching clips of drag queens. In school, it's calling it out when people say "Urgh, that's so gay," or something else queerphobic. It's exploring what you do in your own behaviour which might carry accidental homophobia (for example, "Ew! I could never kiss another girl! Gross!"), challenging the people around us when they say things which are close-minded or outdated and showing up. As an ally, if you've got a friend who is queer, be there for them, listen to their fears and concerns, make sure they know you're there to support them and you are a safe person for them to turn to.

What does an ally do?

Take a minute to think about what you're actually, proactively doing to support LGBTQ+ people.

- Whether you know them or not, if you see or hear someone being made fun of, are you speaking up or is your silence deafening?
- When you're with friends and your unfunny mate tells another gay joke, are you challenging them or are you just not responding?
- When the phrase "that's so gay!" gets thrown about, are you challenging them or are you letting it slide in a way you'd never let someone say "that's so Black" or "that's so Jewish" as a way of meaning something bad?
- If somebody is outed or gossiped about, are you indulging in the gossip and spreading rumours or putting it to bed with a "so what?" and expecting better of your friends.
- When considering what television show to watch, do you think about what kind of jokes the characters make or what message their storylines are sending? Do you stop watching it if hosts or characters say homophobic or transphobic things? When you think about how much you like other celebrities, are you considering their behaviour and the things they've said?

- If a problematic relative is going off on one about how "everything's too liberal these days" are you just letting them dominate and set the tone or are you making it clear that no, you don't agree, and speaking about people in derogatory ways is not OK?
- If you have siblings, cousins or friends who may be LGBTQ+, are you helping to make sure that they know they are free to be themselves and express themselves however they like around you? And that you love and support them unconditionally?
- Are you actively creating a safe space that your friends can go to and be their authentic selves, knowing they can trust you and that you'll never share their secrets or judge them?

I apologize if you found the last few paragraphs confronting, uncomfortable or challenging. Self-reflection is often very uncomfortable. Thank you for sticking with it. We need to be able to have uncomfortable conversations to get anywhere. The starting point of doing better is always reflecting on how well we're doing now. But I also want to clarify – if you found yourself awkwardly recognizing that you might be guilty of some of those behaviours, I don't blame you. I don't think you're a bad person. I don't believe there is a single person on this earth who isn't at least 0.1 per cent homophobic – even LGBTQ+ people can be, and are, homophobic or transphobic. All of us are a little bit because it's how we were raised. But that's not an excuse and it's up to us to educate ourselves and do better.

Education plays a huge part in becoming a great ally. The first step (and it's a continual process) is to educate yourself – and you're already doing that! So, whether or not you already knew that when you picked up this book, you've already taken a great step forward and I'm so pleased to have you on this journey with us – your friends and siblings will be too.

What is not allyship?

Being an ally is not a fixed status, one that you achieve once and then get to not think about again. It is something that must be consistently practised, regardless of who is around us. Allyship is not a party trick, something you perform in front of us and other people for praise. Being an ally is something you do when we're not in the room and, even more importantly, when you're then the odd one out for calling out queerphobic behaviour.

Being an ally is not a title you can award yourself, it is earned and given to you by those you support. Importantly, it's also not an opportunity to put yourself in the spotlight. Think of it like this: in most films and TV shows queer characters are sidelined and become "the gay best friend" and are just a token. But this is our film, we're the main characters and a good ally is a supporting cast member.

Power and privilege

Without allyship, what is friendship and support of the LGBTQ+ people around you? Being neutral is only an option for people with privilege and power. There is nothing inherently wrong with having that privilege or power, that isn't your fault as you didn't decide to have it (just as we didn't decide to be queer) – but what you do with it is your decision.

Whatever the equality and rights movement, it needs allies, but they cannot be centred within the conversation, otherwise a space and a movement designed to bring greater power to a minority can quickly become a place where that minority is once again marginalized and made a side feature in their own story. All too often this happens to LGBTQ+ people – in particular to women, people of colour and trans people as sexism and racism are still social issues within the LGTBQ+ world.

The important thing for an ally to do is to use their inherent power and privilege to help others. Don't change the narrative of our story to build up your part or get more lines. Instead, please tell our stories and share our stories. Use your voice, your power, for that. Echo us, don't talk over us.

Writer and activist Scarlett Curtis's piece that follows is aptly called 'Not my story'. What she touches on, very bravely as it's not easy to admit, is that it can be really difficult to know when it's time to speak up, and when it's time to stay quiet so as to let someone else speak.

Not my story

Written by **Scarlett Curtis**

Having a gay best friend doesn't change the fact that one in five LGBTQ+ people have experienced a hate crime or incident because of their sexual orientation and/or gender identity in the last twelve months. Because friendship without allyship does nothing.

Waving a rainbow flag doesn't help change the reality that 72 countries criminalize same-sex relationships, that the death penalty is allowed as punishment for LGBTQ+ people in more than eight countries, that the average life expectancy of trans women in the Americas is between 30 and 35. Because showing up to Pride, without showing up for action, does nothing.

Asking to be congratulated for being an ally is like asking for a prize for not kicking a dog in the street. It shouldn't be, and should never have been, something to be congratulated for; it should be the norm. And that's where we come in, or where we don't come in, because this isn't really, and has never been, our story.

By "us" I mean those of us who don't identify as LGBTQ+ but have the deep, beautiful and incredible gift of living in a world alongside those who do. By "us" I mean those of us who have fucked up royally in the past as part of society. By "us" I mean those of us who have a lot to apologize for. By "us" I mean those of us who need to be reading this book more than anyone.

Human beings love stories, we always have. More than stories, we love being the centre of stories. Our souls live nestled within weird and wonderful subjective brains. Subjectivity is a magical thing – it gives us empathy, confidence, power, opinions and individuality. It also means that when we encounter a narrative that doesn't concern us, we tend to find it hard to comprehend.

The story of the LGBTQ+ community is a love story written across time, space and history. It is a story of power, oppression and some of the bravest, most wonderful people who have ever existed. It is the story of Gertrude Stein, Bayard Rustin, Virginia Woolf, Harvey Milk, Lady Phyll, Alexis Caught, Munroe Bergdorf and Charlie Craggs. It is the story of my best friend, my greatest teacher, my hero, my family, my idol. But it's not my story and that's a fact that's taken me a little bit of time to get my head around.

I'm still working on it; I'm still figuring it out. I'm still trying to listen and learn and develop tools to be the most powerful ally that I can be. I still make mistakes. I'm vowing to try harder.

What I do know is that the second you start to feel that your allyship has power, the second you place yourself within this story, you are reinforcing systems that have placed you in a position of power as the majority for the past 2,000 years. Privilege is not an insult, it's a fact. Allyship is not a virtue it's a necessity.

You (me) are not a part of this story, and you (me) never really have been. But you (me) do have power, you didn't choose to have that power but you have it as a result of your identity and the one duty you do have is to use that power for good. You are not a part of this story but you can *read* it. And you can give it, wrapped up in a rainbow ribbon, to others who need it.

Looking after you: how to HALT a confrontation

Sometimes, we get stuff wrong. That's part of being human, none of us are perfect – it doesn't excuse bad actions or mean it's OK, but it means it's understandable to slip up sometimes. There's also a time when conversations can get very heated, whether we're under fire for something we've accidentally said or done which has caused offence or whether we're going to bat for our queer friends and siblings and calling out problematic behaviours. Standing up for others can feel like the right thing to do but full-blown arguments rarely achieve anything positive, people only get defensive and we say even worse things in the heat of the moment. Whether you feel under fire or you're calling somebody out, before things go too far HALT and check:

Hungry: none of us are at our best when we're hungry. "Hanger" is a real thing and it's because our physical state overrides our emotional one – hunger, exhaustion and pain all unsettle our emotions. If you're finding it really hard to emotionally regulate yourself in this state or if you feel like you're overreacting, check if this is perhaps fuelled by your physical state rather than emotional.

Angry: check in with yourself and ask, what is fuelling your anger? Or what is it that you're actually feeling? If you're coming under fire, is this anger actually fuelled by shame and embarrassment at being called out? Is it fear of losing someone or being challenged? Try and identify your emotions and where they're coming from so you can have a better resolution.

Lonely: Feeling abandoned is horrible and strikes a knife deep into our emotions and vulnerability. When we feel like we've done something wrong or we're being criticized, it can make us feel really lonely or rejected and we lash out in response to fear and pain. It doesn't make it OK but if we can be aware of this it means we're less likely to do it again.

Tired: Whether we're physically tired or emotionally tired – because we've been worn down from multiple aggressions or arguments and so we overreact to something – we tend to react too strongly in ways that can be out of proportion. Ask yourself, are you tired? Again, name your emotions. "I'm sorry, I'm not handling this well, I'm really tired."

If a conversation devolves into a confrontation, HALT before you say something you'll regret.

But I'm not a "straight ally"? I'm LGBTQ+

Fantastic! Me too! But I've learned that, despite my membership to the best club there is, I need to be consistently aware of both my own place within the LGBTQ+ spectrum and my privilege.

Let me explain – I'm a gay man and I grew up under the homophobia of Section 28. I've been gay-bashed and hospitalized, had romantic and cute moments ruined by homophobic slurs shouted from passing cars, but I present as a gay *man*, and men are still protected and afforded a higher status than women by our patriarchal society. As a man, I am statistically much less at risk of physical threat than LGBTQ+ women. On top of that, while I consider myself to fall into the non-binary spectrum, visibly I pass as very cisgender, and while homophobic hate crimes do happen, these are less common than transphobic violence. On top of all of this, even my race protects me – being white, I am protected from structural racism which impacts queer people of colour on top of any homophobia they may also face.

Years of queers

Section 28 also banned "the promotion of homosexuality". This meant that schools, doctors, nurses, etc., couldn't mention homosexuality – books like this were illegal to have and a teacher could have been banned from teaching if they taught anything about LGBTQ+ identities.

Sadly, even within a minority community, built upon campaigning for love, equality and acceptance, there is still racism and misogyny which affect queer women and people of colour. They can often be marginalized within our own community. It's especially important that we challenge racism, sexism and transphobia within queer spaces, otherwise our LGBTQ+ siblings can end up as a "double minority": rejected by both sides and embraced by none. We want to be a place where everyone is welcome, equal and free to be themselves with no judgement. That's how you can be an ally to others in our community, even if you're LGBTQ+.

Sure, a Black lesbian and I both have to come out and navigate homophobia – but how that homophobia affects us will be different. I may be able to relate to many other queer people through our shared common experiences, as people who are not part of the heterosexual, cisgendered mainstream, and that may give me *some* understanding of what their journey and lived experience might be like, but it will never match up to the full thing.

Only by listening and considering what we have in common and our differences, and fighting for equality for all of us, can we ever stand unified. As an LGBTQ+ person, you can be an ally. Think of it as stepping in to back up your sibling, sure, you may not be totally alike and disagree on some things, but nobody messes with your family.

afterword

I hope that this book has been helpful for you, and that it really has inspired you to think about who you are and who you hope to be as you grow and evolve throughout life – something we should always be open to.

I started off this book by saying that even though I'm writing this I don't have it all figured out, I'm just a little bit further along in my journey than you. Figuring ourselves out is a life's work, and so now I leave you with the remarkable words of someone I admire, cherish and respect both for what a wonderfully kind human he is and for the representation he has given our community – Russell T Davies.

Again, Russell is a little bit further along the yellow brick road in his exploration of the self (you don't mind me saying that Russell, right? I'm still invited to dinner, right?!) and he *still* doesn't profess to have it all figured out, to have all the answers and to never face challenges. A man who (in his own words) has been out as "professionally gay" for years still has moments of uncertainty – so don't feel like you're alone in this, it happens to the best of us, and to all of us. Here are Russell's words...

Coming out

Written by **Russell T Davies**

I come out every day.

Many years ago, I wrote a drama for ITV called *Bob &
Rose*. In one scene, Bob said, "You don't just come out once,
it's not like on TV where you stand up and make a speech
in the Queen Vic. It happens every day. With everyone you
meet. And it never bloody stops."

I was right, at least for me. The coming out keeps on
coming. It's not a problem at work; I'm lucky that I've written
a lot of gay stuff which acts as a flag in front of me, a great
big pink flag entering the room before I do, all big and
clumsy and bold. Just how I like it.

But work is only a tiny part of the day. For the rest of
the time, I'm left wondering. With every new person. Every
shop. Every smile. There it is, that little voice, ticking away,
that tiny nag at the back of my head whispering, "Do they
know? Can they tell? Am I visible? Should I say? Why?
Why not?" Questions which ask essentially: who am I?
On and on and on.

I entered a whole new intricate dance back in 2011.
My boyfriend, Andrew, was diagnosed with a Grade 4
brain tumour. That's as bad as it gets. There is no Grade 5.
But the fight began. He started treatment, which became a
non-stop carnival of seven craniotomies with a wild funfair
of side-effects: epilepsy, a stroke, drug-induced diabetes,
hydrocephalus, hormone deficiency. At one point, he was
even strapped to a giant, yellow metal spirit level in case he
tilted his head one degree above the horizontal.

We lived right next door to the biggest hospital in Manchester, but just our luck, the neurology department is way across town, in Salford. I've never learned to drive (it terrifies me, I think drivers are geniuses) and Andrew's epilepsy meant he had to surrender his driving licence. So when he was hospitalized for months on end, I had to rely on taxis.

Ah, yes. The subtle art of coming out to a taxi driver.

I'd visit in the day, go back home, visit in the evening, go back home, four trips a day. As a result, over hundreds of journeys, from a random pool of black cab drivers – invariably male, I can't remember a woman ever driving – I got to know a core of 30 or 40 drivers. And they were nice, they were chatty, they'd ask why I was going to the hospital every day. And then I had a choice:

My friend is ill.

My boyfriend is ill.

Which one do you choose?

Well, boyfriend, obviously. Except. Every time? Must I?

I'd sit in that taxi and be wary of the word boyfriend. Wary of the driver's response. And wary of mine because, if the word provoked a reaction I didn't like, could I leave? If I suspected a glance, a sneer, a raised eyebrow, would I let it go? And if I did, how defeated would I feel? How disappointed in myself? That essential question, still demanding to know: who am I? And yes, I was stereotyping the drivers, although they did live up to the archetype.

Middle-aged and straight, always.

I confess. Every now and then, I'd say that Andrew was just my friend. I'm as out as out can be, and yet, trapped inside that black metal box, I found that I didn't always have the strength. Or the nerve. Or I just couldn't be arsed! Sometimes, I didn't want to be that man, with his flag, his cause, his politics. I was tired and scared, and the journey was fraught, I'd be carrying washing, and shoes, and food and messages. Bags full of things, things for sickness. Rehearsing stories in my head, tales of the outside world, to keep Andrew entertained. And it was important to arrive at that hospital not vexed, but happy, so he'd see a smiling face.

So don't make me come out. Not now. Not four times a day. Not when he's dying. Please.

And then I'd be ashamed. Of myself, of my failure, of my compromise, of my presumptions. Of my racism, even, if the taxi driver was Muslim and I avoided an encounter with a little more precision.

All of this going on in my head, unspoken, as we trundled through Manchester. Winter and summer, sunshine and rain. Skyscrapers and cranes rising up around us. Me, lost in thought, a gay man in his 50s still wondering how out to be.

The journeys went on and on. Andrew's fight was successful, for an astonishing amount of time. A prognosis of eighteen months stretched into many years, to everyone's joy. He tricked me into marriage in 2012 (yeah, that old "I might not have long to live" routine) and two of the taxi drivers, ones I'd told the truth to, drove us to the registry office. "No charge!" Those wonderful men.

But in my evident need to complicate things, the happy day gave me a new word to battle with. "My husband is ill." Did I have to say that now? At the same time, a whole raft of drivers, puzzled by the closeness of two men, drifted towards a completely different conclusion. They'd ask, "How's your brother?" Dear God, try unpicking that. "He's not..." Oh, sod it. "He's fine!"

Your lies catch you out, of course. Andrew came home for long stretches – years on end, eventually – and I'd accompany him to his hundreds of medical appointments with the same taxi drivers, now delighted at how well he looked. But I hadn't kept score! I couldn't remember to whom I'd said what. I'd stare at the back of a taxi driver's head, thinking: did I tell him friend, or boyfriend, or husband? And Andrew was a fantastically uncomplicated man, blissfully unaware of my nonsense, so he'd sit there happily chatting away. If he mentioned our wedding, I'd suffer a sharp little jolt. Wrong driver! Hush!

The good luck ran out in the end. The cancer came back in new and vengeful forms. It even took the shape of water. And he died ... he died.

In the hours immediately after his death, I had to confront a new and terrifying world of men and cars. The body, the funeral, the hearse. Thank God for my friend Phil, who gave me the greatest gift of my life: the number of a gay funeral director. I cannot tell you the immensity of the relief. No euphemisms, no doubt, no compromise. The worst of days became bearable, because that little voice in the back of my head was silenced. Andrew and I were out, in death.

Today, six months later, I face a whole new form of coming out. Every time I get into a taxi, and one of those 30 or 40 drivers rolls around, the jolly question comes, "How's your friend?" And now I'm ashamed when I tell them he's gone. These men I never quite trusted, oh, their dismay, their horror, their kindness. Their love. One driver had to pull the car over and have a little cry at the wheel, with me, sitting in the back, mortified at not knowing whether he's crying over my friend or my boyfriend or my husband or my brother.

It's still not over. There are still drivers who haven't popped up yet on the rota. So I wait. They'll come. Give it time. But for now, I like those men, best of all. They're the ones who think he's still alive.

But when they ask, I'm certain now that I will tell them the truth. It took his death for me to finally realize a very simple truth. To come out is not a statement of politics. It is an act of love.

And I'll move on. Still coming out. Every day, every chat, every person. Maybe it never ends. But without him, I discover that the question is louder than ever: who am I now?

As Russell asks who is he now – I turn to the question of this book, who are any of us, and importantly, who do we want to be?

I hope this book has helped you answer some questions and ask inspiring new ones.

But if we can be anything, be ...

honest
loving
daring
out
passionate
proud
open
queer
happy
patient
powerful
respectful
kind
compassionate
admirable

you

brave
pioneering
genuine
joyful
nurturing
thoughtful
shining
strong
charitable
tender
outspoken
resilient
challenging
heartfelt
generous

resources
and support
services

Shout 85258 mental health advice for young people

shout
85258
here for you 24/7

If you are feeling worried, stressed, overwhelmed or low, you are not alone. We have some practical tips and techniques you can try to help you feel calmer.

- **Take a break:** When you're dealing with a lot of different things, it can become overwhelming. Taking a break can help, whether that's getting away from your screen for a few minutes, going for a walk or taking some time off. Be kind to yourself for all that you are managing right now.
- **Make time for self-care:** Set aside time for yourself to do small things that can have a positive impact on your mental well-being, such as reading, cooking, watching a film or meditating. Whatever you do, make sure it's something that you want to do and that makes you feel good.
- **Get creative:** Sometimes writing down how you feel can help you take control of your feelings when you can't find the words to say out loud. Some people find journaling helpful, while others may choose to express their feelings through poetry, song lyrics, drawing or scrapbooking.
- **Get moving:** Whatever your level of fitness, exercise can help to improve your mood and enhance your mental well-being. Even a 10-minute walk can help.

- **Listen to music:** Music can have a powerful effect on well-being. It can boost your mood, remind you of a particular time in your life, make you want to dance around or help you unwind and relax into sleep.
- **Create a sleep routine:** Well-being and sleep go hand-in-hand. Sleep resets our ability to be focused, motivated and emotionally stable. Around eight hours of sleep a night is key but sometimes it can be hard to get enough good-quality sleep. Creating a sleep routine is the first step. Get into bed at a reasonable hour in the evening and wake up at the same time every morning, even on the weekends.

If you are struggling to cope, Shout 85258 is only a text message away. We are here to support you 24/7 with any mental health concerns you are experiencing, including anxiety, depression, suicidal thoughts, loneliness, relationships, sexuality, racism, bullying and body image.

Anyone in the UK can **text 'SHOUT' to 85258** anonymously, confidentially and for free to speak to a trained volunteer any time of the day or night.

If your life is at imminent risk, please call 999 for immediate help.

For more ways to manage your mental health, visit **giveusashout.org**.

Staying safe online

Whilst the Internet is full of useful info, you also need to be sensible about exploring life online. There are a few simple things you can do to help keep you safe online.

- **Privacy:** Make sure that you use high privacy settings on social networks.
  Personal information: Don't give out personal information online. This means you should not share your home address, school name or telephone number. Remember, just because someone asks for information about you does not mean you have to tell them anything about yourself!
- **Screen name:** When creating your screen name, do not include personal information like your last name or date of birth.
- **Passwords:** Don't share your password with anyone but your parents. When you use a public computer at school make sure you log out of the accounts you've accessed before you leave.
- **Photos and videos:** Think carefully before you upload things online. Once it's uploaded, it's no longer private and could be viewed by friends, family, teachers and strangers.

- **Online friends:** Unfortunately, sometimes people pretend to be people they aren't. Remember that not everything you read online is true. If you do want to meet someone you've met online, it would be best to have a video call with the person first and let your parents know. When you meet up, take one of your parents with you and meet in a public place. If they are who they say they are, they'll be happy to do this.
- **Bullying:** Don't send or respond to mean or insulting messages. Tell someone if you receive one. If something happens online that makes you feel uncomfortable, talk to your parents or to a trusted adult, such as a teacher at school. You can also block anyone on social networks that you've had contact with that was negative or unsafe so they can no longer contact you or view your profile.
- **Social networking:** Many social networking websites have minimum age requirements to sign up. These requirements are there to protect you!

Resources and support services

Places to go for more information or to seek support:

General support and mental health services for children and young people

- **Childline**: childline.org.uk, or call 0800 11 11 for the 24/7 helpline for children and young people
  Advice and support for children and young people under eighteen on home, school, relationships and more
- **YoungMinds**: youngminds.org.uk
  Mental health support for children, young people and their parents
- **Mindout**: mindout.org.uk
  Mental health support for the LGBTQ+ community
- **The Mix**: themix.org.uk
  A signposting service for anyone under 25, with advice and support for children and young people on home, school, relationships and more
- **Ditch the Label**: ditchthelabel.org
  An anti-bullying charity supporting young people aged 12–25

LGBTQ+ youth organizations

- **Stonewall Youth**: stonewallyouth.org
  Youth-led organization that empowers young LGBTQ+ people
- **The Proud Trust**: theproudtrust.org
  An organization that supports young LGBTQ+ across the UK through youth groups and other social programmes

- **UK Black Pride**: ukblackpride.org.uk
  UK Black Pride is Europe's largest celebration for LGBTQ+
  people of African, Asian, Caribbean, Middle Eastern and
  Latin American descent
- **National Student Pride**: studentpride.co.uk
  Organizers of the UK's biggest LGBTQ+ student event

Gender and sexuality

- **Stonewall**: stonewall.org.uk
  General information about gender and sexuality, and advice and
  support for the LGBTQ+ community
- **Mermaids**: mermaidsuk.org.uk. Call 0808 801 0400 for the
  helpline, open Monday–Friday, 9am–9pm
  Support for transgender, non-binary and gender-diverse children
  and young people. They also work with parents and carers of
  young people going through these feelings
- **Mindline Trans+**: mindlinetrans.org.uk, or call 0300 330 5468
  Monday–Friday, 8pm–12am (midnight)
  A helpline run by and for trans, non-binary, gender-diverse and
  gender-fluid people. The service is also available for friends and
  families of trans+ people in need of support and advice. Calls are
  occasionally answered by cisgender allies
- **Gendered Intelligence**: genderedintelligence.co.uk
  A charity working to share information about gender diversity
  and supporting young people who identify as trans
- **Switchboard**: switchboard.lgbt. Call 0300 330 0630 for the
  helpline, open every day 10am–10pm
  LGBTQ+ helpline available seven days a week
- **Not A Phase**: notaphase.org
  A charity Supporting the lives of trans+ adults across the UK

Relationships and personal safety

- **Galop**: galop.org.uk, or call 0800 999 5428 for the National LGBTQ+ Domestic Abuse helpline or 020 7704 2040 for the LGBTQ+ Hate Crime helpline
  Support for all LGBTQ+ people who've experienced hate crime, domestic abuse or sexual violence
- **AKT (Albert Kennedy Trust)**: akt.org.uk
  Supports LGBTQ+ people aged 16–25 in the UK who are affected by homelessness or living in a hostile environment
- **National Domestic Abuse Helpline**: nationaldahelpline.org.uk, or call 0808 2000 247
  Free 24/7 helpline for women and children

Sexual health

- **Terrence Higgins Trust**: tht.org.uk/hiv-and-sexual-health/sexual-health/improving-your-sexual-health
  Information and advice about HIV and sexual health. This is the main section of their website dedicated to advising LGBTQ+ people about sex and sexual health
- **LGBT Foundation**: lgbt.foundation/sexualhealth
  Advice on lots of different topics for LGBTQ+ people. This is the main section of their website dedicated to sexual health
- **NHS sexual health pages**: nhs.uk/live-well/sexual-health
- **NHS sexual health services**: nhs.uk/service-search/sexual-health (search for your nearest sexual health clinic)
- **PrEPster**: prepster.info
  Team PrEPster offer information on PrEP (pre-exposure prophylaxis) medicine for the prevention of HIV
- **GMFA (the gay men's health project)**: gmfa.org.uk
  Information and advice on sexual health and well-being for gay, bisexual and trans men

Reporting online issues

- **Report Harmful Content**: reportharmfulcontent.com
  Advice and support around reporting threats, harassment,
  bullying and other harmful content online
- **Report Remove**: childline.org.uk/info-advice/bullying-abuse-
  safety/online-mobile-safety/remove-nude-image-shared-online
  of you has been shared online, you can report it and get support
  removing it

Advice for parents and teachers

- **Stonewall**: stonewall.org.uk/help-advice/coming-out/coming-
  out-advice-and-guidance-parents
  Stonewall also offer advice to parents and family members
- **FFLAG (Families and Friends of Lesbians and Gays)**:
  www.fflag.org.uk, or call 0845 652 0311
  A national charity who offer help and support to parents and their
  LGBTQ+ children
- **Schools Out**: schools-out.org.uk
  A charity campaigning to make UK schools and educational
  institutions safe spaces for LGBTQ+ communities for everyone
  from teachers to pupils
- **LGBT+ History Month**: lgbthistorymonth.org.uk for
  A charity helping to increase the visibility of LGBTQ+ people
  – their history, lives and their experiences – in the curriculum
  and culture of educational and other institutions and the wider
  community
- **The Classroom**: the-classroom.org.uk
  An online resource created to help teachers include the LGBTQ+
  experience in their lessons. Resources are free to download and
  site users can also upload their own

Religious support groups

- **Hidayah LGBT+**: hidayahlgbt.com
  Providing support, education and welfare for the Muslim LGBTQ+ community
- **Diverse Church**: diversechurch.website
  A charity offering advice and support for LGBTQ+ Christians
- **Sarbat**: sarbat.net
  A organization for LGBTQ+ Sikhs
- **KeshetUK**: keshetuk.org
  Support and advice for LGBTQ+ Jews and Jewish communities
- **Gaysians**: gaysians.org
  Support and resources for the South Asian LGBTQ+ community
- **House of Rainbow**: houseofrainbow.org
  Fosters relationships among Black, Asian, Minority Ethnic (BAME) LGBTQ+ people of faith

acknowledgements

Acknowledgements

I have a lot of people to thank in this book, because it's been a long road to get here and a lot of people have helped, given time, given feedback and given kindness to get this book (and me) to where it is today. There is no way I could have a logical order for this so, in no particular order, here goes.

To all of the contributors, THANK YOU for your generosity of spirit, kindness and openness when you gifted me your words to add to this book. THANK YOU.

John Moore, I wouldn't have got through the doors at Walker Books if it weren't for you, THANK YOU. Walker has been a wonderful place to find as my publishing home, and to my two brilliant editors, Daisy Jellicoe and Charlie Wilson, THANK YOU for taking some very raw work and a very fledgling writer and giving me encouragement, feedback, space and your time. THANK YOU, Jamie Hammond, for designing such a brilliant book. To the rest of the *Queer Up* Walker family – Marketing, PR, Schools and Libraries, Sales – THANK YOU, this is a group effort quite literally not possible without you.

Hannah Weatherill and Martin Redfern, my literary agents at Northbank, THANK YOU. Hannah, thank you for helping to pivot the original proposal and rework it for a new audience. Martin, thank you for taking a random punt and seeing the start of an idea.

Guy Warren-Thomas, Ogechi Ofoegbu, Lucy Chaloner, Jonathan Poole and the rest of the team at M&C Saatchi Social, THANK YOU for taking me in, accepting when I say "no" more than "yes" and my scepticism at some of this world. Guy, above all, thank you for your patience and your friendship in this.

Charlotte Walker, I wouldn't even be in these places if you hadn't generously given me some of your time to listen to my confusion and insecurities and helped me get to a place of understanding – let alone opening your contact book for me. THANK YOU.

Callum McSwiggan, you are so wonderfully rare in that you genuinely look to help out other people rather than working on a quid pro quo basis, THANK YOU. You introduced me to Michelle Ellman, THANK YOU, Michelle, you gave me encouragement and some of your infectious energy and introduced me to Scarlett. Scarlett Curtis, THANK YOU for not just your words in this book, but for including me in *It's Not OK to Feel Blue* and being generous with your platform.

Qmmunity podcast team – EVERYBODY involved, Christania and Char, Kevin, Renay, Laura, Effie, Rez – I learned a lot from you all in many different ways. And each of you, I thank for it all.

Shout family, thank you for always making our crisis resolution team a friendly, fun and accepting place to be. No matter the time of day, and no matter what conversations we're having, there is always somebody there. It's a brilliant organization, made up of brilliant people, THANK YOU for having me as part of it.

My clinical home and my supervisors, Dr Karen, Dr Mike, thank you for welcoming me into the practice and giving me so much generosity. THANK YOU.

The Breakfast Club, Áine and Mike, having you as my companions in my psychotherapeutic training has just been such a blessing. THANK YOU.

My coven of Bog Witches, Abi, Ana, Jess, it's not often that you meet people who accept you and embrace you so wholeheartedly. We may not be together physically all of the time, but I love you all so dearly and THANK YOU for being part of my life.

Kevin, thank you for your patience and guidance. THANK YOU.

LuSo, our friendship has taught me so much, THANK YOU.

The Gays, Dillon, Sam, Brennan, Dudley, Sam, Chris, Owen and Jeremy, Jocky, Tom, Luke and Dom. THANK YOU.

Simon Davis, Matt Webb, Eden Hannam and the Kings Cross Steelers for building me a home in rugby, THANK YOU. My new home, the Hunters, THANK YOU for being so welcoming.

Miss Moss and Mrs McNamara, geezus, school was rough and that was a difficult time, but you two went far beyond the role of teacher and quite literally kept me alive. THANK YOU.

Charlie Craggs and Kuchenga Shenje, I adore you both so much, you are wonderful, wonderful human beings. THANK YOU.

My extended blended family, you have all taught me lessons for this book and that family is what we make of it, THANK YOU for having me as your brother, uncle and godfather to your kids.

My parents – who knew having three English teachers as parents would turn into a book? – thank you for always sending me back to redo my homework, for giving me a love of words and language, for never telling me off for always asking "why?" and encouraging me. THANK YOU, I love you. I hope I make you proud.

To you, dear reader, **THANK YOU** x

This book is dedicated to you, to the child in me, who we may grow to be and those who never got to love and be free.

A.C.